JOSEPH UNROBED

Holding on to Your Dreams When Life Seems Like a Nightmare

MARK BARNARD

Unless otherwise noted:

Scripture quotations taken from the New American Standard Bible®, Copyright © 1960, 1962, 1963, 1968, 1971, 1972, 1973,1975, 1977, 1995 by The Lockman Foundation Used by permission. (www.Lockman.org)

Copyright © 2016 Mark Barnard

All rights reserved. This book or parts thereof may not be reproduced in any form, stored in any retrieval system, or transmitted in any form by any means—electronic, mechanical, photocopy, recording, or otherwise—without prior written permission of the author, except as provided by United States of America copyright law.

For permissions contact info@blessingpoint.org

Blessing Point Ministries
703 Waterwood Bend
Peachtree City, GA 30269

ISBN-13:978-1523736300
ISBN-10:1523736305

DEDICATION

To those who find themselves wandering in the field of life.

CONTENTS

	Preface	7
	Introduction	9
1	Clothing Does Not Always Make the Best Gift	15
2	Always Remember to Take Your Coat!	35
3	Expensive Clothes Become Affordable When Someone Else Pays for Them	53
4	Disguises Sometimes Come in Handy	73
5	Returns Are Easier If You Have Your Receipt	85
6	Some Styles Are More Forgiving than Others	99
7	When You Have Nothing Left to Wear	119
8	Updating Your Personal Wardrobe	135
	Additional Resources	155
	Acknowledgements	169

PREFACE

The idea for *Joseph Unrobed* has dogged my mind for more than a decade. I hesitated to pursue it because earlier studies on Joseph's life noted his famous robe but missed the other clothing references in his story. I found this hard to believe and wondered why no one had picked up on it. *Multiple* garments associated with Joseph hide in plain sight and I build upon that theme. I recently discovered one author who used a similar approach, but that book takes on a fictional style.

I take a biblically based expositional approach to Joseph's life. However, not everything I describe is as obvious in the Joseph narrative as I'd like. Some of what I bring out flows from the context, particularly his family dynamics. This includes my assertion that Joseph wrestled with self-importance in the first half of his life. Evidence for this arises from the Bible's record by implication rather than stated fact. Many readers get the impression that Joseph grappled with pride in the beginning of his story. While that may be true, the perception arises from *between* the lines of Scripture. However, the applications I draw from his implied shortcomings are clearly substantiated by other parts of the Bible. Passages that address God's sanctifying work in His people, and His loving discipline of them, undergird the points I make.

When studying the life of someone like Joseph, in one of the Bible's historical books, three things unfold at the same time. First, the record describes God's workings in the lives of people in the narrative itself. Second, the narrative reveals part of God's larger redemptive plan for mankind through the ages. Third, the Holy Spirit applies the passage to our lives as we ponder its personal relevance. *Joseph Unrobed* emphasizes what God was doing in key biblical figures and what He may be saying to us through their experiences. While His redemptive plan for the ages forms the backdrop of this book, my emphasis focuses on the personal relevance of Joseph's saga.

Joseph Unrobed does not explore the typology usually associated with this story. Other authors have covered the similarities between Joseph and Jesus Christ. Neither is this an academic work. It is designed to be practical. I explore how God healed Joseph from traumatic injuries, and freed him of particular traits, before using him in the way He planned. God attempts the same work of healing and preparation in our lives, equipping us for our role of greatest usefulness. My hope is that readers will recognize how this plays out in their lives and begin to see painful circumstances in a new light.

MRB

INTRODUCTION

I trudged up the hill known as Ann Street. I dreaded the trip to the Department of Family and Children Services (DFACS) located at its peak. A few minutes earlier I had returned home from school and found myself locked out of our house. With the security chain fastened from the inside, the front door would only open a few inches. When I yelled, for my mom to let me in, she screamed through the narrow opening, *"Who are you? You're not my son!"* I knew by the twisted look on her face that she had once again broken with reality. I immediately foresaw she would be admitted to Greystone, the regional mental hospital. I knew my younger brothers and I would be placed in foster care. It had happened before.

I made my way into the DFACS office and found the receptionist. The office was familiar. I had been there before with my mother when she would periodically go to fill out paperwork to keep our welfare checks and food stamps flowing. On this visit, at the age of twelve, I explained to our case worker that my mom had stopped taking her medication and needed help. My younger brothers and I needed protection too. When she got into this state of mind there was no telling what she would do. I sometimes wonder that I survived my childhood.

My father abandoned the family when I was seven and we moved several times until finally settling in the three story apartment at 64 Market Street. What went on inside that apartment shaped (or, perhaps better, misshaped) me. I struggled daily with an amplified sense of emptiness, intensified by my family's circumstances. If I happened to find a scrap of joy, despair devoured it before I could. The shame of living in poverty made the back of my neck tighten. My neck was tight a lot. The whole experience left me angry and sullen. Though I knew how to behave around teachers and parents, privately I demonstrated many of the "acting out" behaviors typically found in wounded souls.

At the age of fifteen I began a personal relationship with Jesus Christ and my life made a significant course change. A radical experience of God's love and forgiveness provided the first measure of healing in my life. However, recovering from deep-seated wounds experienced in my family of origin, would take a lifetime.

Perhaps my traumatic childhood drew me to the Bible's many stories of troubled families and how God worked in their midst. Some of the greatest biblical characters came from families pockmarked by painful events. We sometimes glamorize biblical figures while ignoring the challenges that shaped their lives. Gideon overcame fear of his family's reprisals. Young Samuel found his calling while living apart from his parents. Ruth's faith took root in the rocky soil of widowhood. Jonah's reluctant obedience revealed ingrained and perhaps inherited prejudice.

Even Joseph, whose story we explore, couldn't claim perfection. Many authors paint Joseph as a man of flawless character. I take a different tact. Informed by the Bible's teaching on the depravity of man, I don't see Joseph as sinless. Nuances of Joseph's failings whisper to us from the pages of his story. His flaws largely grew out of his father's favoritism, self-importance tainting the first half of his life. I'm glad it did. Joseph's story gives the rest of us hope. That hope grows out of the tangled roots of family and fallen-ness, brothers and betrayal.

You may already be familiar with the story of Joseph. He's a character in the Old Testament, famous for his *coat of many colors*. But there's more to his story than just that one coat. Several references to clothing surface in Joseph's story. In addition to his famous coat, he leaves a cloak in the clutches of the sinister Mrs. Potiphar. He later abandons his prison clothes and exchanges them for a royal robe. At one point he adorns a disguise to hide his identity. When his brothers tear their clothes in grief, Joseph comforts them and offers each a set of new clothes. In the end, Joseph has nothing left to wear. He simply asks that his bones be transported back to the Promised Land, when the Israelites make their escape from Egypt centuries later.

These clothing references help us understand the progression of God's work in Joseph's life. Each garment gets mentioned at a point of transition. Most of the transitions tend to be painful. Each article of clothing bears similar meaning too, like the symbolism we might associate with a king's robes or a policeman's uniform. Joseph's clothing speaks of his stature and importance in each stage of his journey.

The symbolism tied to Joseph's clothing arises from the

narrative itself. The coat of many colors represents Joseph's elevated standing among his brothers. The cloak Mrs. Potiphar uses as evidence against Joseph changes his standing in Potiphar's household. The prison clothes he wore speak of his standing (or lack of it) as an inmate in Pharaoh's jail. The robe gifted him by Pharaoh speaks of Joseph's standing at court. The disguise Joseph wears conceals his elevated position from his brothers. The clothing Joseph later offers his brothers represents reconciliation, elevating his brothers' standing. Joseph's ultimate standing as a member of God's family gets symbolized in his request that his bones be removed from Egypt centuries later, at the exile.

I believe God still speaks to us through such symbols. He speaks generally ("The heavens declare the glory of God" - Psalm 19) and sometimes specifically. He arranges events and circumstances to get our attention about particular things in our lives, usually about painful issues which we have ignored. We need eyes to see and ears to hear the meaning of such providential signposts, not to mention the confirming voice of others to endorse our interpretation of them.

Joseph's trail of strewn clothing takes us on a journey from woundedness to reconciliation and from nightmare to dream come true. It's an epic story of how God heals and uses broken people. Such stories get written every day in the lives of millions of Christ followers. Like the exposed roots of a tree toppled in a storm, the roots of many people's lives prove insufficient for the strong winds of life. God actively works to heal the gnarly roots of our lives.

INTRODUCTION

Just like Joseph, His work often consists of a pattern of painful events designed to get us to address the underlying damage in our hearts.

Perhaps by the end of the book you'll agree that a symbolic pattern does exist. You may recognize it in Joseph's story and perhaps in your own life too. If so, you may need to exchange your clothes like Joseph did. The uncomfortable garments of the past often hang on us like the weight I felt trudging up Ann Street. My prayer is that God sets you free from what weighs *you* down and that the nightmares you have faced will fade as His dreams for you become reality.

MRB

Chapter 1

Clothing Does Not Always Make the Best Gift
Genesis 37

"Now Israel loved Joseph more than any other of his sons, because he was the son of his old age. And he made him a robe of many colors . . . So when Joseph came to his brothers, they stripped him of his robe, the robe of many colors that he wore." (Genesis 37:3, 23 ESV)

"Play with me! Play with me!" I yelled, as my dad headed down the stairs. Getting my father to play with me was my last ditch attempt to keep him from abandoning our family. At the age of seven I knew he was leaving. As he made his way toward the front door, my desperate cries followed. My pleading, however, proved vain. My dad walked out the door and my dream of a loving family faded into a nightmare of hurt. Like time released poison, devastation dispensed a steady stream of rage into my system. Rage unleashed a desire for revenge. Vengeance aroused every nerve ending in my body. I didn't know how I'd do it, but someday. . . *I'd get even.*

Sadly, an epidemic of woundedness, like mine, spreads through our culture daily. Less than half of American children now live in a traditional two parent heterosexual family. One third live with a single parent. Another fifteen percent live with two parents, one or both being remarried. Five percent of all children live with grandparents or with no parents at all.[1] In place of the traditional family, which dominated American life fifty years ago, dysfunction has become the new normal.

Based on those statistics, there's a good chance you have your own gut wrenching story of familial pain. You may harbor your own thoughts of getting even. If only those who cause such wounds would think through their actions! If only many of us didn't have to live with the emotional hangover of being discarded, abandoned, abused, or neglected. Yet countless individuals go through life as angry victims. In many cases, their emotional systems have blown a fuse because of someone's thoughtless, selfish, and sometimes evil acts.

The story of Joseph begins with a well-intentioned deed that caused massive pain in his family. If only Jacob had thought through the implications of giving an ostentatious robe to his younger son. This one action ripped the relational fabric of his family, the damage lasting for decades. And believe me, *his other sons got even!*

In later episodes, articles of clothing continue to play a crucial role in Joseph's life: the cloak he leaves behind in the hand of Potiphar's wife, the prison clothes he wears when incarcerated, the garments of fine linen Pharaoh places upon him, the changes of clothes he gifts his brothers upon their reconciliation, and, in the

---

[1] Gretchen Livingston, "Fewer than half of U.S. kids today live in a 'traditional' family" http://www.pewresearch.org, (December 22, 2014).

end, Joseph's has nothing left to wear. He simply requests the Israelites take his bones from Egypt when on route to the Promised Land.

I don't believe the record of Joseph's strewn clothing is an accident. I believe God designed the references to Joseph's various robes to show us how He worked in Joseph's life, healing him from painful wounds and preparing him for the future. It appears that most of God's work in Joseph's life involves the *pain* of stripping off what he no longer needs. Joseph gets stripped of his clothing at least three times. On each occasion, he has to leave something behind, something he thinks useful, but in reality, hinders God's ability to use him.

Joseph's trail of clothing provides a glimpse into the way God works in our lives too, healing and preparing us, often through a pattern of painful events. Just as God used pain to shape Joseph, He uses pain to draw our attention to wounds He longs to heal. If we fail to respond to the shaping influence of pain, God mercifully causes us to face further crises, because He wants us to get over any hindering issues from our past. Unless we address the wounds stopping our growth, they will hold us back from the deep experience of healing necessary to be totally free—the objective God seeks.

God facilitates this deeper work in a person's life though he or she may have never made the connection. It took Joseph a while to realize what God was doing too. His story starts in Genesis chapter thirty-seven.

[1] Now Jacob lived in the land where his father had sojourned, in the land of Canaan. [2] These are the records of the generations of Jacob. Joseph, when seventeen years of age, was pasturing the flock with his brothers while he was still a youth, along with the sons of Bilhah and the sons of Zilpah, his father's wives. And Joseph brought back a bad report about them to their father. [3] Now Israel loved Joseph more than all his sons, because he was the son of his old age; and he made him a varicolored tunic. [4] His brothers saw that their father loved him more than all his brothers; and so they hated him and could not speak to him on friendly terms. [5] Then Joseph had a dream, and when he told it to his brothers, they hated him even more. [6] He said to them, "Please listen to this dream which I have had; [7] for behold, we were binding sheaves in the field, and lo, my sheaf rose up and also stood erect; and behold, your sheaves gathered around and bowed down to my sheaf." [8] Then his brothers said to him, "Are you actually going to reign over us? Or are you really going to rule over us?" So they hated him even more for his dreams and for his words. [9] Now he had still another dream, and related it to his brothers, and said, "Lo, I have had still another dream; and behold, the sun and the moon and eleven stars were bowing down to me." [10] He related it to his father and to his brothers; and his father rebuked him and said to him, "What is this dream that you have had? Shall I and your mother and your brothers actually come to bow ourselves down before you to the ground?" [11] His brothers were jealous of him, but his father kept the saying in mind.

Despite Our Roots

Even with the widespread woundedness in our day, the painful relational dynamics in Joseph's family surpass those found in many modern households. Let's explore how various parties played into his family's problems. How did this web of relationships become so tangled? How did emotions become so charged? We get an inside look at Joseph's family system and *it's not pretty.*

The Brothers' Hatred

Notice how intense feelings become among Joseph's siblings. The word *hate* gets repeated three times to describe their collective attitude toward their kid brother: "And his brothers saw that their father loved him more than all his brothers; and so they hated him and could not speak to him on friendly terms" (vs. 4); "they hated him even more" (vs. 5); "So they hated him even more for his dreams and for his words" (vs. 8).

Joseph's brothers experienced the emotional sting of being less loved and couldn't stand Joseph because of it. It's interesting that they take their anger out on Joseph and not their father, with whom the problem started. Perhaps it seemed easier to blame Joseph than ascribe fault to their father whose love they desperately craved. As a result, the brothers seethe with disdain for Joseph. The gift of the robe and Joseph's dreams infuriate them. The brothers, who have long wrestled with suppressed rage, soon prove unable to restrain their fury.

Joseph's Contribution

Did Joseph contribute to the problem? We can only guess what motivated him to bring his father the bad report about his brothers, but he puts himself at odds with his siblings from the second verse of the story! Before his father gives him the fancy frock, before he dreams his dreams, Joseph finds himself on the outs with his brothers, a group notorious for their ruthlessness.[2] And did he really help himself by making his second dream public? Did he not see their reaction to his first dream? Was he rubbing it in? Did he feel no sense of danger in sharing his second dream? Joseph plays right into his brothers' hostility.

Joseph's immaturity doesn't help matters. He was seventeen years old when the story begins. Think about that. How many seventeen year old males think they know all the answers? How much more so if your ego gets inflated by your father's favoritism? Could any teenager handle promotion without becoming cocky or conceited? Joseph faced an unmanageable challenge. With little experience, he must cope with his father's favoritism and his brother's feelings of revulsion toward it.

The Favoritism Dynamic

How did Jacob's favoritism impact the family? Were Joseph's brothers right to loath the robe and all it represented? Don't we feel resentful when we sense that one of our peers enjoys special privilege? "What's so great about them?" we might wonder. Are we jealous, coveting their favor for ourselves? Maybe. Joseph's brothers certainly gave into envy. But most people recognize a fundamental unfairness imbedded in the concept of favoritism.

I once taught Middle School for a year, eighth grade to be specific. One day, I allowed a certain student a privilege which I

---

[2] See Genesis 34 to learn just how ruthless Joseph's brothers could be.

had denied others. As soon as I granted it, another student piped up, *"Hey, why did you let him do that and you wouldn't let me?"* I made the mistake of sarcastically responding, "Because I like him better!" It may have been a joke to me, but to the student posing the question there was nothing funny about it. He immediately replied, *"That's obnoxious!"* He was right. Something basic to our sense of fairness knows that favoritism feels obnoxious. Now, imagine being on the short end of favoritism for seventeen years! That's how Joseph's brothers felt. They had to watch him parade around in his obnoxious robe. They had to put up with his obnoxious dreams. They could barely tolerate his obnoxious presence.

Jacob and His Wives

What about Jacob? Jacob, also known as Israel, starts the trouble in verse three, "Now Israel loved Joseph more than all his sons, because he was the son of his old age." Let's stop there a moment. Jacob had two wives: Rachel and Leah. He also bore children with two women named Zilpah and Bilhah, servants of his wives. A husband with the equivalent of four wives makes for big problems! Years ago, while visiting Israel, I asked our tour bus driver if he knew anyone with more than one wife. He replied soberly, "Yes, I have a friend with four wives." He went on to say, "My friend also has four headaches!"

Jacob suffered his share of headaches largely because of the pecking order among his spouses and their children. Jacob loved Rachel dearly. He got tricked into marrying Leah by his uncle. His feelings toward Zilpah and Bilhah go unrecorded in Scripture, but we safely assume his affection for them failed to reach the heights of his love for Rachel. Leah and Rachel's competition for Jacob's attention fostered jealousy and hard feelings that set up Joseph's brothers' hatred of him.[3]

Why does Joseph enjoy favored status? He was the oldest son of Jacob's most beloved wife.[4] In fact, Jacob may have viewed Rachel as his only *true* wife.[5] Later in the narrative Judah quotes his father as saying, "You know that my wife bore me two sons."[6] He says this of Rachel in regard to Joseph and his full brother Benjamin. If Jacob viewed Rachel as his only true wife, he could see Joseph as his oldest son and rightful heir. This would be the case even if his half-brothers were born before him. Additionally, Rachel suffered with infertility for many years prior to giving birth to Joseph. Her barrenness explains Jacob's old age at Joseph's birth and why Joseph was seen as someone special from the day he was born.

The Robe of Rivalry

The second half of verse three goes on to describe just how special Jacob thought Joseph was: "and he made him a varicolored tunic." The word "tunic" has largely lost its place in our vocabulary today. Other translations use the word "robe." This gift

---

[3] Genesis 30
[4] Mathew Henry, Mathew Henry's Commentary on the Whole Bible, Volume 1 (USA: Hendrickson Publishers, 1996) 169.
[5] C.F. Keil & F. Delitzsch, *Commentary on the Old Testament, The Pentat*euch (Grand Rapids, MI: Eerdmans, 1989) 365.
[6] Genesis 44:27; 46:19

of clothing bears tremendous symbolic meaning to the rest of the family. For us today, it would be like one sibling getting the lion's share of his or her parent's estate. The gift communicates not only how Jacob feels about Joseph but also how he feels about his other sons.

The contrast between Joseph in his fancy robe and the clothing his brothers wore was striking. His brothers wore clothing suited to shepherds working in the field. Their garments went down to the knees, the sleeves cut off at the shoulder. Their clothes served a purely practical purpose geared toward the hard work of tending livestock.

Now, think of the wealthy Arab sheiks we see on television from time to time, the ones who own all the oil. Think about their long flowing robes. Each one dresses as a prince. Usually their robes are clean and white, trimmed in gold. Their robes are a sign of privilege, of wealth, and of royalty. That's the kind of robe Jacob made for Joseph, though perhaps more ornate. Joseph's robe set him apart as a prince among his brothers. His robe meant that he, not they, stood at the head of the family line.

What about the fact that the Bible says Jacob *made him* a varicolored tunic? If Jacob had the garment made for Joseph, it would have been bad enough. Here Scripture suggests that his father had a hand in actually sewing it together. How that would have *grieved* his brothers! Not only had Jacob given him the thing, but he possibly made it himself. His father was either clueless to the effect the robe would have on the rest of the family, or he just didn't care. How obnoxious!

In summary, we have a father who loves one child more than his other kids. We have a favored son with a clumsy knack for setting his brothers off. We have ten male siblings with a seething hatred for one of their own. And, to top it all, we have four silent mothers! (None of them play a role in the story.)

Finding Meaning in the Mess

Can we find any comfort in the opening scene of Joseph's story, as messy as it is? Yes, here it is: God works in and through Joseph's family, one blended in the worst of ways. Instead of seeking a healthier family to use for His purposes, God sticks by Jacob's clan. We should find solace in the fact that no matter how imperfect, convoluted, abusive, or hate filled a family might be, God's remains available to them. This assumes that you know how Joseph's story ends. As painful as this story starts, it ends amazingly well.

Joseph is not the only one with a painful family background. There may have been times of great pain in your family, among siblings or parents. Right now, you may long for your family to get some kind of help. Don't give up hope. God often works in wounded families by reaching into them and producing surprising outcomes. Your family may even go to church, or have a special relationship with God, like Joseph's family did. Joseph's family enjoyed a unique relationship with God that went back several generations. We learn from this that even families like Joseph's, ones that try to honor God, can suffer serious relational problems.

If you see your family as less than ideal, remember how God reached into Joseph's family. Unstable, difficult, and wounded families are often a garden where healing takes root. And God's particular plan for you, in the midst of your family, may unfold in an unexpected way, just as Joseph's life turns on the following unexpected encounter.

Life's So Called Chance Encounters

The following verses always amaze me. The day starts off in such ordinary fashion. Joseph's brothers are out taking care of the flocks and his dad wants to know how they are doing. So Jacob sends Joseph to check on them. The assignment seems ordinary enough until Joseph arrives at his brothers' intended destination and finds them missing. The rest of Joseph's life hinges on the following "chance" encounter.

> [12] Then his brothers went to pasture their father's flock in Shechem. [13] Israel said to Joseph, 'Are not your brothers pasturing *the flock* in Shechem? Come, and I will send you to them.' And he said to him, 'I will go.' [14] Then he said to him, 'Go now and see about the welfare of your brothers and the welfare of the flock, and bring word back to me.' So he sent him from the valley of Hebron, and he came to Shechem. [15] A man found him, and behold, he was wandering in the field; and the man asked him, 'What are you looking for?' [16] He said, 'I am looking for my brothers; please tell me where they are pasturing *the flock*.' [17] Then the man said, 'They have moved from here; for I heard *them* say, 'Let us go to Dothan.'' So Joseph went after his brothers and found them at Dothan.

Some say Shechem was located twelve miles from Joseph's home base at Hebron, others suggest it was as far as sixty miles. In either case, it suggests the nomadic lifestyle embraced by those entrusted with the care of flocks. Shepherds tended to move around, camping under the stars in the best location that afforded grazing and water for the animals. But when Joseph arrives at Shechem, his brothers are nowhere to be found. Out of ideas, about what to do next, Joseph was "wandering in the field."

Now things get interesting. A stranger finds Joseph wandering in the field and offers help. This same stranger *just happens to have heard* his brothers say they were going to Dothan. What are the odds of that happening, and why would a chance encounter with a stranger be recorded in Scripture? If this stranger were not on-site, Joseph would never have found his brothers. He would have likely given up looking and headed home. He would never have been sold to Egypt, never been put in an Egyptian prison, and never exalted to second in command under Pharaoh!

We see these kinds of "chance" encounters elsewhere in the Bible. We watch one occur in Abraham's life. Just as he raises the knife to sacrifice his son Isaac, God stops him and, at the same time, a ram gets stuck in a nearby thicket (Genesis 22). The ram takes Isaacs' place on the altar of sacrifice. We see another chance encounter in the story of Ruth when she just happens to collect produce from the field of Boaz, a distant relative and her future husband (Ruth 2:3). At the death of Ahab in 2 Chronicles 18:33, a man "drew his bow at random" and just happened to hit the king in the gap of his armor, and killed him! Some would call it a "lucky shot," a coincidence. Just such a seeming coincidence changes the entire course of Joseph's life.

What does Joseph's chance encounter with a helpful stranger mean for him and for us? God leads people even as they wander, unsure of what to do next! It means God works out his plan for each of us through means we might not at first recognize. For God to fulfill his plan for Joseph, He had to get Joseph away from his family. He had to separate Joseph from his privileged rank. Getting Joseph out of his comfortable position, out of his beautiful robe, would take a significant event. That event arises from Joseph wandering in a field and a chance encounter with a helpful stranger. Crazy, but true!

When Joseph later languishes in prison, he probably wished he had never met the man in the field! When he became second in command of all Egypt, he likely felt otherwise. If you think you will never get to the place God wants you to be, remember the stranger in the field. If you are anxious to get to the next stage of your life, relax. God will get you there, and it will likely be through circumstances that seem as "lucky" as Joseph's stranger.

Life changes quickly for Joseph, on several occasions. Each upheaval brings him closer to becoming the man God wanted him to be, in the position God envisioned for him. God fulfilled Joseph's dreams using periodic shifts of location and standing. Some of the transitions look more like nightmares than the dreams of exaltation Joseph envisioned. One of those nightmares begins in the next painful scene. A scene that starts a humbling work in Joseph's life, a life *without* his famous coat.

Humiliation and God's Plan for Your Life

Understanding humility reminds me of trying to grip a fist full of Jell-O. As soon as you apply pressure, it slips through your fingers. The more I realize how prideful I really am the more I need better definitions of humility.

Humiliation, on the other hand, creates a lasting impression. We all know what humiliation feels like. Experience humiliation once, and you never forget it. The flush in your face, the sudden awareness of your fault, and the public exposure of your mistake emblazons the experience on your mind. Humiliation hurts. Humiliation *angers.* Yet, humiliation, if we embrace it, can teach us important lessons. The humiliation Joseph experienced flowed from the humiliation his brothers felt for the previous seventeen years. They lived at the bottom of the pecking order. Joseph, younger yet most favored, resided at the top. His brothers hoped to reverse that ranking. They devised a plan to deal with their brother, the "dreamer."

> [18] When they saw him from a distance and before he came close to them, they plotted against him to put him to death. [19] They said to one another, 'Here comes this dreamer! [20] Now then, come and let us kill him and throw him into one of the pits; and we will say, 'A wild beast devoured him.' Then let us see what will become of his dreams!' [21] But Reuben heard *this* and rescued him out of their hands and said, 'Let us not take his life.' [22] Reuben further said to them, 'Shed no blood. Throw him into this pit that is in the wilderness, but do not lay hands

CLOTHING DOES NOT ALWAYS MAKE THE BEST GIFT

on him'—that he might rescue him out of their hands, to restore him to his father. 23 So it came about, when Joseph reached his brothers that they stripped Joseph of his tunic, the varicolored tunic that was on him; 24 and they took him and threw him into the pit. Now the pit was empty, without any water in it. 25 Then they sat down to eat a meal. And as they raised their eyes and looked, behold, a caravan of Ishmaelites was coming from Gilead, with their camels bearing aromatic gum and balm and myrrh, on their way to bring *them* down to Egypt. 26 Judah said to his brothers, "What profit is it for us to kill our brother and cover up his blood? 27 Come and let us sell him to the Ishmaelites and not lay our hands on him, for he is our brother, our *own* flesh." And his brothers listened *to him.* 28 Then some Midianite traders passed by, so they pulled *him* up and lifted Joseph out of the pit, and sold him to the Ishmaelites for twenty *shekels* of silver. Thus they brought Joseph into Egypt. 29 Now Reuben returned to the pit, and behold, Joseph was not in the pit; so he tore his garments. 30 He returned to his brothers and said, 'The boy is not *there*; as for me, where am I to go?' 31 So they took Joseph's tunic, and slaughtered a male goat and dipped the tunic in the blood; 32 and they sent the varicolored tunic and brought it to their father and said, 'We found this; please examine *it* to *see* whether it is your son's tunic or not.' 33 Then he examined it and said, 'It is my son's tunic. A wild beast has devoured him; Joseph has surely been torn to pieces!' 34 So Jacob tore his clothes, and put sackcloth on his loins and mourned for his son many days. 35 Then all his sons and all his daughters arose to comfort him, but he refused to be comforted. And he said, 'Surely I will go down to Sheol in mourning for my son.' So his father wept for him. 36 Meanwhile, the Midianites sold him in Egypt to Potiphar, Pharaoh's officer, the captain of the bodyguard.

Here's how the scene plays out. Without the restraining influence of their father's presence, his brothers immediately hatch a plan to *kill* Joseph. We watch Ruben, who had issues of his own,[7] save Joseph from death. We witness his brothers strip the despised robe from Joseph and throw him into a dry cistern. We see another chance encounter, as the Ishmaelite caravan arrives at just the right moment. We learn of Judah's pragmatic leadership in suggesting they sell their brother off to a foreign land. We watch Joseph get shipped off. We witness colluding sons intentionally deceive their father. We cringe at the shallow comfort offered Jacob by the sons who betrayed him.

Jacob's expression of love, in his gift of clothing to Joseph, backfired. His other sons hated Joseph's robe. Verse 23 says, "they stripped Joseph of his tunic, the varicolored tunic that was on him." The robe represented all that his brothers despised, Joseph's rank in the family and in their father's heart. Joseph's famous tunic proved to be a coat of contention, a robe of rivalry. His brothers summarily stripped him of his princely status.

Did Joseph *need* to be humiliated? Perhaps. Reading the early account of Joseph's life, it's not hard to smell the scent of pride attached to his robe. The bad report he brought to his dad, about his brothers, suggests an air of superiority. He shares his dreams of dominion over the family without concern about how it would impact his brothers. The fact that he was seventeen years old when this story begins suggests a degree of immaturity. His father's favoritism, so obvious to the rest of the family, would set up any young man for a fall. Could he wear that special robe, dressed so

---

[7] Genesis 35:22

differently from his brothers, without a consciousness of how it set him apart? If Joseph did not carry some degree of self-importance, his brothers could easily project it on him. The evidence suggests, that while God had plans to exalt Joseph in the future, He needed to humble him in the present.

The humiliation Joseph experienced was not gentle. Years later, when his brothers reflect on their actions, we learn more about what Joseph went through, "Then they said to one another, Truly we are guilty concerning our brother, because we saw the distress of his soul when he pleaded with us, yet we would not listen" (Genesis 42:21). Their recollection betrays how emotionally charged the scene of Joseph's removal from Canaan was. In spite of his distress and pleadings, Joseph's life gets forcibly turned upside down. What a nightmare.

In Joseph's story, we see a number of things happening all at once. Joseph's character gets shaped, humiliation chipping away at pride. We note that his brothers have pent up issues of their own, which need to be healed. We see God moving Joseph toward the life that He has in mind for him, in Egypt. In the riveting account of Joseph's betrayal we glimpse both harm and hope. The harm jumps off the page. The hope, more subtle, winks at us from between the lines of Scripture. We know how the story ends, though Joseph lingers in the dark for now.

Another Seventeen Year Old

At age seventeen and freshly graduated from High School, I

got a job at a car dealership across the street from my house. I worked for the parts department, driving a brand new GMC pickup truck. I delivered car parts to various auto shops in the area. I loved my job. It made me feel important. I harbored no thought of going to college.

Then, a series of events took place that changed the course of my life. In all of about two weeks, I had three small accidents in the company truck. None of them were my fault, at least that's what I told myself. The first accident involved another car that pulled out of a parking space and into my vehicle. In my inexperience, I failed to get insurance information from the other party. I endured an uncomfortable meeting with the dealership's owner to explain what happened. He graciously instructed me on the proper way to document an accident. In a few short days, I would need that advice when I found myself in a second car accident! Once again, the boss forgave me, but I was getting nervous. I wondered at my worsening driving record and how it affected my job security.

Not long after the second accident, I managed to get a four inch diameter light post wedged between the truck's thick wooden push bumper and front right fender. For the life of me, I can't explain how I got the truck in that position in the first place! In a state of sweaty panic, I eventually maneuvered the truck free of the pole but not without leaving a two foot long dent in the brand new truck. I felt sick and scared. I drove around town looking for an auto shop that might quickly pull out the dent. It was not to be. Too embarrassed to go back to work, I dropped off the truck without explanation and never returned. Events sometimes conspire to so humiliate us that we willingly leave behind that which we thought we could never part with.

Not long afterwards, someone gave me an application to college. I felt no sense of direction, but, upon the flip of a coin, filled out the free application. Miraculously, I was accepted! (If you saw my high school transcripts, you'd understand why it was miraculous.) When I got to campus, I felt a strong sense of confirmation that I was where I was supposed to be. It was there that I met my wife and trained for my vocation. I grew as a person at that school.

While in college I started to become aware, too, of how early wounds in my life were affecting me. I had no remedies at this point, but I began to sense that my heart was more like one of stone than the living center of my being. As I got away from my home, I gained the space I needed to recognize my condition. None of that would have happened had there not been three minor traffic accidents and some accompanying humiliation. Did I see the good that would come from quitting my job at the dealership? Not likely. Do I humbly thank God for forcibly moving me in a new direction – absolutely!

We need to accept the humiliation life thrusts on us, even if it means having something we value stripped from us. It may catapult us onto God's path for our life. It's the path Jesus trod. The Bible tells us, "He . . . emptied Himself, taking the form of a bond-servant . . . Being found in appearance as a man, He humbled Himself by becoming obedient to the point of death, even death on a cross."[8] Humiliation may lead you to the next step in God's plan. Resist it, and, like Joseph does, you may have to face it again.

Chapter 1 – Study/Discussion Questions:

1. How would you describe your relationship with your parents and siblings?
2. Has a chance encounter ever changed your plans?
3. To what degree have painful situations impacted your life?
4. How does humiliation feel to you; how would you describe it?
5. Has God ever used humiliation to change the direction of your life?
6. How does humiliation foster greater spirituality?

---

[8] Philippians 2:7-8

Chapter 2

Always Remember to Take Your Coat!
Genesis 39

"She caught him by his garment, saying, "Lie with me!" And he left his garment in her hand and fled, and went outside" (Genesis 39:12).

In the Fall of my fifteenth year, my life took a dramatic turn. I had witnessed two of my friends become Christians. They seemed to find peace and shed many of their so called "sinful" behaviors. Their life changing experiences intrigued me. I hungered for meaning in life. I needed relief for the guilt I felt over my destructive behaviors too. The more I hung around them, I became convinced that what my friends possessed was real. One night, while walking down the street in Madison, NJ, I prayed. I'm not sure it really counted as a prayer. I didn't ask for anything. I told Jesus something. I said, "Lord, I give you everything." Now when you tell God that you "give him everything," He perks up! Turns out He's looking for people willing to do just that.

I didn't have much to offer, just the mess that was my life. Jesus took that mess and filled me with joy, right there on the street! The next day, I lost three quarters of my vocabulary. Not because of some new moral code to which I had to adhere, but because He removed the profanity. My frequent nightmares vanished. The haunting fear of death evaporated. He filled my emptiness with a new vibe, one that stirred to tell others about Jesus.

I started attending a church with some of my friends. I plugged into the youth group and began reading the Bible. I grew in my faith and made new friends who encouraged me. Things were going great. But then something happened that threatened to sidetrack everything. It happened at church. And like Joseph, it involved clothing.

Picture the scene. My untamed hair, tinted eyeglasses, and a somewhat hardened background (think Steven Hyde from "That Seventies Show") showing up at a small traditional church. They sang hymns. I preferred rock. They were older. I was fifteen. They came to church dressed in suits and ties. I wore cut-off jeans and a tee shirt with the phrase "Keep on Trustin'" emblazoned on the front. The phrase was a Christian version of a popular saying back then – "Keep on Truckin'."

I attended this church for months unaware that my cut-off jeans made some of my senior brethren uncomfortable. One day a church leader approached me. He offered to take me shopping for some new clothes. When I think of how things could have gone down, I'm amazed at how well they turned out. Instead of offering to take me shopping, this church leader could have made a stink – demanding that I dress nicer for church. He might have told me to find a different church! I could have been offended and chosen to abandon church, labeling them superficial Pharisees. Instead, I told him "thank you" and we went shopping for new jeans. Who knew clothing could be a problem, one that challenges the hearts of God's people?

In the next phase of Joseph's life, he faces a crisis, over clothing, *again!* What this crisis reveals about Joseph's heart proves both encouraging and daunting. The way Joseph responds to difficulty teaches us that we can make progress in one area of life, while lagging behind in another. Both progression and regression occur as we grow into the role God envisions for us. You will experience failures and successes as you advance toward the dream God puts in your heart. And when another unexpected crisis occurs, as it does for Joseph, it may feel like your dream will never materialize. Here is how Joseph's second clothing controversy unfolds.

> [1] Now Joseph had been taken down to Egypt; and Potiphar, an Egyptian officer of Pharaoh, the captain of the bodyguard, bought him from the Ishmaelites, who had taken him down there. [2] The LORD was with Joseph, so he became a successful man. And he was in the house of his master, the Egyptian. [3] Now his master saw that the LORD was with him and *how* the LORD caused all that he did to prosper in his hand. [4] So Joseph found favor in his sight and became his personal servant; and he made him overseer over his house, and all that he owned he put in his charge. [5] It came about that from the time he made him overseer in his house and over all that he owned, the LORD blessed the Egyptian's house on account of Joseph; thus the LORD'S blessing was upon all that he owned, in the house and in the field. [6] So he left everything he owned in Joseph's charge; and with him *there* he did not concern himself with anything except the food which he ate.

The Back Story

This phase of his Joseph's life contains challenges most people would find overwhelming. We want to explore the challenges Joseph faced, in his transition to life in Egypt, because they form the back story to his second clothing crisis.

Sold off by his brothers back in Canaan, Potiphar, one of Pharaoh's officials, purchases Joseph as a slave in Egypt. The account of Joseph's advancement in Potiphar's service, God's blessing on his work, the indecent proposal by Potiphar's wife, and Joseph's subsequent incarceration, flows so effortlessly one gets the impression all this transpired within six months. However, Genesis 39 occupies a long period of time. We learn from Genesis 37:2 that Joseph was seventeen when his story begins. We know from Genesis 41:46 that he received his promotion from Pharaoh at the age of thirty. Allowing for the time he spends in prison, the intervening years in Potiphar's service could represent as much as a decade.

Let's start at the beginning of that near decade spent as a slave. What challenges did Joseph face when arriving in Egypt? He encounters an entirely foreign culture. He must learn a new language. As a slave, he has no rights, no privilege, no rank, and no say. The faith he grew up with would be tested by a different religious system. Joseph, no doubt, wrestled with his feelings over what happened to him at the hands of his brothers. In his loneliness, doubts would creep in like termites, eating away at his God inspired dreams.

This must have been one tough adjustment. Dwelling on the injustice of his situation, Joseph could have nursed a rebellious attitude. It would have been easy to find reasons to resist or undermine his new master. An escape attempt was not beyond reason. But the summary found in Genesis 39:1-6 suggests none of this. Rather, the story to this point reveals something in Joseph well beyond his years – the *submission* of his will.

Submission of the Will

What went on in Joseph's heart during this transition? The way the favor of God drapes this passage, we must assume that Joseph put his heart in a bless-able state. God's favor is mentioned or alluded to five times! That blessing manifested itself in Joseph's competence as Potiphar's right hand man. Everything he managed turned into a success. What a comfort that must have been to Joseph. At least something was going right in his life. As successful as he was, Potiphar must have thought he had won the lottery by acquiring Joseph as a slave.

Joseph, likely, wrestles with his displacement, but he does not let it interfere with his new role. Verse two says, "And he was in the house of his master, the Egyptian." That simple statement tells us more than where Joseph slept at night. No slave would be housed in close proximity to his master unless first proven trustworthy. The phrase tells us that Joseph served Potiphar in a manner that demonstrated dependability.

Few fare as well when they feel the sting of injustice like

Joseph did. Facing circumstances we neither choose nor desire can sour us toward God and others. When painful circumstances are thrust upon us, how can we keep from developing a hard heart?

Think about David's plea for a *willing* spirit in Psalms 51:12, where he wrestles with the consequences of his adultery with his neighbor's wife Bathsheba. David had Uriah, Bathsheba's husband, murdered as a cover up for his sin. When he finally comes clean, David prays, "Restore to me the joy of Thy salvation, and sustain me with a *willing spirit*." (Italics mine.) Why does David pray for a "willing spirit?" Because sin never softens an offender's heart. As long as it stays hidden or un-confessed, sin hardens one's heart. David, realizing the gravity of his offense, prayed that God would protect him from becoming hard hearted about his sin.

Our hearts can also become just as hard when we are sinned *against*. That's the danger that Joseph faced. He may not have sinned like David did, but he was sinned *against*. And the danger of becoming hard hearted was just as real for Joseph as it was for David.

A hard heart closes down communication. We shut ourselves in, others get shut out. We anticipate the next infliction. Protecting ourselves from the next infliction, we seek to control who we let get close to us. Those folks who gain access are few. The greater our hurt, the harder our heart, the harder our heart, the less access is given to who we really are. As a result, we close ourselves off to the world. Hardened. Sullen. Often depressed and critical.

Joseph demonstrates a *willing* spirit. Even though Joseph was gravely sinned against, he willingly trusts God for the future. He goes to work and overcomes challenges. God blesses his efforts and it motivates him to do more. He never takes his anger out on Potiphar, even when he has multiple opportunities to rebel by sleeping with Potiphar's wife. Joseph remains committed to God, even when he doesn't like his circumstances. The Apostle Paul instructed his protégé Timothy, "Let no man look down on your youthfulness, but rather in speech, conduct, love, faith and purity, show yourself an example of those who believe."[9] Joseph sets such an example.

Joseph applies himself to his new job rather than moping or sulking over his low position. We see a young man who makes the most of a miserable situation and appears to receive a series of promotions because of it. Verse four suggests a progression in Joseph's level of responsibility. He starts out as a slave in general and then becomes Potiphar's personal servant. Next he is made overseer of Potiphar's house, then finally, Potiphar puts all that he owns under Joseph's charge! Verse six tells us that Potiphar puts so much faith in Joseph that he does not concern himself with any of Joseph's decisions. The only thing Potiphar handled himself was meal planning. As I mentioned earlier, this takes place over about a ten year period.

Just as Joseph had found favor with his own father, he finds it again with Potiphar. Just as his father had elevated him, Potiphar

---

[9] 1 Timothy 4:12

does the same. We are about to discover, with shockingly similar symbolism, a callous household member seeks to undo all that good, and another article of clothing proves harmful to Joseph's health.

Seduction of the Will

> Now Joseph was handsome in form and appearance. [7] It came about after these events that his master's wife looked with desire at Joseph, and she said, "Lie with me." [8] But he refused and said to his master's wife, "Behold, with me *here*, my master does not concern himself with anything in the house, and he has put all that he owns in my charge. [9] There is no one greater in this house than I, and he has withheld nothing from me except you, because you are his wife. How then could I do this great evil and sin against God?" [10] As she spoke to Joseph day after day, he did not listen to her to lie beside her *or* be with her. [11] Now it happened one day that he went into the house to do his work, and none of the men of the household was there inside. [12] She caught him by his garment, saying, "Lie with me!" And he left his garment in her hand and fled, and went outside. [13] When she saw that he had left his garment in her hand and had fled outside, [14] she called to the men of her household and said to them, "See, he has brought in a Hebrew to us to make sport of us; he came in to me to lie with me, and I screamed. [15] When he heard that I raised my voice and screamed, he left his garment beside me and fled and went outside." [16] So she left his garment beside her until his master came home. [17] Then she spoke to him with these words, "The Hebrew slave, whom you brought to us, came in to me to make sport of me; [18] and as I raised my voice and screamed, he left his garment beside me and fled outside."

It turns out Potiphar was not the only person to appreciate Joseph. Mrs. Potiphar eyed him for her own uses. Joseph, with all his administrative duties, must have found time to work out. The Bible tells us he "was handsome in form and appearance." With time on her hands, and little to do around the house, Mrs. Potiphar began to solicit Joseph for sex. A lesser man would have given in to her seduction. If Joseph's heart had been fixed on advancement, he could have slept his way to greater influence. Far from home, and no doubt lonely, he could have easily indulged his boss's wife. However, when it came to sexual temptation, Joseph kept his *clothes* on!

Notice how Joseph describes the indecent proposal made to him, "Why should I do this great evil and sin against God?" How did Joseph come to recognize adultery as "evil and a sin against God?" Joseph's faith accompanied him to Egypt! We safely assume that Joseph learned to fear the Lord at his father's knee. We also note that Joseph experienced betrayal, first hand, through his brothers. He knew the pain he'd cause Potiphar if he slept with his wife. If we think back a little further, we recall the turmoil caused by his oldest brother Rueben. Ruben slept with his father's concubine Bilhah (Genesis 35:22). Joseph likely knew this painful story and had no interest in repeating it. No doubt Joseph also recalled the chaos when Shechem took advantage of his sister Dinah (Genesis 34). His brothers exacted harsh vengeance on the men of Shechem over the same kind of sin Mrs. Potiphar was now suggesting.

Joseph's convictions and his acquaintance with the consequences of unrestrained lust led him to refuse Mrs. Potiphar.

Unimpressed with Joseph's stance, she hounded him daily none-the-less to the point where Joseph had to avoid her. He saw through her evil intentions.

A Lesson about Evil

How well do you recognize evil? Potiphar's wife hands us a crash course in how to identify evil when its shadow crosses our path. Mrs. Potiphar's seductions reveal that evil can appear appealing *when it suits its purposes*. Her refrain of "lie with me" reveals evil's desire to unite with, and even possess its victims. That she would not drop the subject, but pursued Joseph, "day after day," betrays evil's incessant nature. We also witness the willful and manipulative disposition of evil in the way Mrs. Potiphar implicated her husband as the cause of her troubles, "See he has brought in a Hebrew to make sport of us . . . (vs. 14)." Who is the "he" she refers to? It's her husband. She does it again in verse seventeen, "The Hebrew slave who you brought to us . . ." Who is the "you" she speaks of? Her husband, Potiphar!

Evil also subverts the truth with plausible lies as revealed in the temptress's words in verse fifteen, "When he heard that I raised my voice and screamed, he left his garment beside me and fled and went outside." Since she could not seduce Joseph, Mrs. Potiphar uses a half-truth to reframe her guilt as his. Evil never hesitates to destroy good people to obscure suspicion about itself. Her effort to frame Joseph might have led to his death, and she knew it! The spurned and hateful Mrs. Potiphar reminds us that evil's allure always masks darker intentions and potentially deadly outcomes.

Faithfulness Comes With a Price

Joseph does a stellar job resisting the ongoing pursuit of Mrs. Potiphar. His example shines especially bright when compared to Judah's misbehavior in the previous chapter. One wonders at Judah's story being placed between the first and second episodes of Joseph's life. The ease with which Judah sleeps with Tamar in Genesis 38 adds luster to Joseph's resistance to seduction in Genesis 39.

But Joseph's faithfulness comes with a price. Though he successfully avoids the trap of adultery he now faces circumstances beyond his control. He resists temptation, but the injustice unfolding around him must feel like déjà vu! There are too many similarities not to notice. As with his brothers, he is at the mercy of those stronger than he. As he was thrown into the cistern, he now faces prison or worse. As he bore the brunt of his brothers' hatred, he now faces vitriol from Mrs. Potiphar. The favor he had enjoyed with his father, Jacob, he experienced with Potiphar. That favor disappears, *again*.

When Potiphar hears his wife's accusation, he responds with anger. We are not told the target of his wrath. It's easy to imagine that losing Joseph as a servant would irritate him in and of itself. Potiphar could have had Joseph executed for attempted rape. As Rueben saved him from death the first time, it's likely Potiphar's doubts about his wife's story save Joseph from the death penalty now. In both cases his clothing plays a key role. If only Joseph had held onto his coat when he hurried out of the house! If he had, there would have been no physical evidence to substantiate Mrs. Potiphar's lie. While Joseph's life unravels again, God is weaving a plan that brings meaning to the painful events he endures.

What If Joseph Had Given In?

Joseph is an example of someone who overcame sexual temptation. That's not always the case. Sometimes we cave in to lust. We give in to temptation. What then? You may be reading Joseph's story with regret. You may want to put the book down, or even, throw it away. Sometimes one person's success reminds us of our failure.

Remember that among the many people in the Bible, only one made it through life without sinning. He was born of a virgin. Unless you have that kind of pedigree, you will eventually give into temptation. I share this not to suggest you have permission to sin but to help you recover, should you do so.

Max Lucado in his book, *On the Anvil*, describes how giving in to sin is like falling through an open manhole. Here's how it works. Satan sneaks up on you with a tempting opportunity. In a moment of weakness you fall into what Lucado calls "sudden sin." However, rather than enjoying the pleasure you thought the temptation would bring you, you lie crumpled in a sewer of guilt and regret.

Lucado describes the various ways we give in to sudden sin. He writes, "You lose your temper. You lust. You fall. You take a drag. You buy a drink. You kiss the woman. You follow the crowd. You rationalize. You say yes. You sign your name. You forget who you are. You walk into her room. You look in the window. You break your promise. You buy the magazine. You lie. You covet. You stomp your feet and demand your way. You deny your Master. It's David disrobing Bathsheba. It's Adam accepting the fruit from Eve. It's Abraham lying about Sarah. It's Peter denying that he ever knew Jesus. It's Noah, drunk and naked in his tent. It's Lot, in bed with his own daughter. It's your worst nightmare. It's sudden. It's sin."[10]

Should you fall into sudden sin, there's only one way out of that dark hole. A promise in the Bible provides an elevator ride out of the dungeon of guilt and regret. In a letter the Apostle John wrote he says, "If we confess our sin, He is faithful and just to forgive us our sin and cleanse us from all unrighteousness."[11] I may have lost three fourths of my vocabulary when I became a Christian, but there were plenty of other areas of life with which I struggled. I failed so often that I sometimes wondered if I'd wear out God's promise of forgiveness and cleansing, if we confess our sins.

If Joseph's story deviates from yours, please don't think he was perfect. We will learn that while Joseph overcomes sexual temptation, he struggles in another area. We all blow it. Please don't languish in your failure, or think that God rejects you because of it. His word says, that if we confess our sin . . . He will forgive us of *all* sin, not some. If you come to Him with a broken

---

[10] Max Lucado, On the Anvil (Wheaton, IL: Tyndale House, 1985) 92-93.
[11] 1 John 1:9

heart, just as we read about David doing earlier, you can be cleansed afresh. Once you get clean again, ask the Lord to guard you from temptation. Stay alert for the uncovered manholes Satan puts in your path!

Sanctification and the will

So far, everywhere he goes, Joseph leaves clothing behind. Why do we find this odd motif running like a news ticker across the screen of Joseph's life? Why would God tag this particular feature in major episodes of crisis, drama and reconciliation? What is the message that God intends us to get through this trail of robes?

Finding Meaning in Joseph's Garments

If symbolic meaning can be attached to the various garments mentioned throughout Joseph's story, what might it be? To his brothers, Joseph's famous coat symbolized preference and standing in the family. To his father, it represented affection, and favor. What did the coat of many colors mean to Joseph?

It may be hard to tell, but when a younger child gets exalted above ten older brothers, it would be impossible for him not to feel a sense of entitlement. The bad report he brought about his brothers predates the robe and may suggest he was already afflicted with a touch of sibling snobbery. His dreams of ruling over his brothers could easily fan the embers of self-importance. One cannot read the account of that first robe without sensing that Joseph, at seventeen, the son of privilege, comes across as being somewhat full of himself. To all the parties involved in the first season of Joseph's life, the coat of many colors symbolized favoritism, status, and being more important than others.

What of the second robe, the one Mrs. Potiphar ripped off of him? Do we sense any of that same self-exalting association? If we read his response to Mrs. Potiphar's advances with emphasis on a few key words, we hear Joseph's self-importance still ringing. "*Behold*, with *me* here, my master does not concern himself with anything in the house, and he has put all that he owns in *my* charge" (Italics mine). What may seem subtle comes out more clearly in his next statement, "There is no one greater in this house than *I* . . ." (Italics mine.). Why did he feel the need to exclaim that? Joseph could do whatever he wanted in Potiphar's service without being challenged in the realm of his influence.[12] Blinded by his status, he fails to recognize that at least one other person in the household carries greater influence than he, Mrs. Potiphar.

In both the first and second episodes of Joseph's life, clothing bore a label we would associate with status. After a while, living for status begins to stink like a pile of dirty socks, like when a kid comes home from summer camp with no socks in his suitcase. His mom asks, "What happened to all those new socks I sent with you to camp?" Her child replies obliviously, "I don't know." The truth be told, those socks were just too stinky to bring home! The account of Joseph's robe from Genesis 37 and the cloak from

---

[12] Frances A. Schaeffer, *No Little People* (Wheaton, IL: Crossway Books, 2003) 97.

Genesis 39 suggest both items were too foul-smelling before God. The robe his brothers stripped from him and the cloak Mrs. Potiphar grasped smelled of the same odor. Once again the symbol of rank and standing had to be removed from Joseph.

The Primary Test

The primary test in this second episode of Joseph's life is not how he responds to Mrs. Potiphar's advances but how he responds to the pride of position. The temptation of adultery reveals the sin of pride. He has yet to be freed from the self-importance he inherited from his family of origin.

Like Joseph, we can beat temptation in one area of life (lust) and at the same time have a weakness in another (pride). God commends the former and in his love holds us accountable for the latter. Joseph succeeds in submitting his will to God during his transition to Egypt and in avoiding Mrs. Potiphar's sexual advances. Yet he overlooks the arrogance in his heart. This teaches us we can submit our wills to God while remaining blind to deeper issues.

What is God doing in Joseph's life? He wants to get Joseph to the location where he needs him (the Egyptian court) with his heart in a state that will not undermine his usability in that position. God's work in Joseph's heart plays out on a tri-parallel track, along with getting him to his occupational destiny and fulfilling God's plan for Israel.

God pursues a similar parallel work in our everyday affairs in order to wean us from traits which limit His use of us. Yet, are we aware of it? Not often. It is much easier to recognize painful patterns in others. How often do you or I stand back and look at the breadth of our lives? God may be speaking, even shouting, to us through repeated painful events, like Joseph with his robes. Yet, we gain little or no discernment.

To help Joseph get free from his overly developed sense of self, God sends him a fresh dose of humiliation in the form of prison time. Being a slave is one thing, having a prison record another. It appears Joseph's career careens in the exact opposite direction of his youthful dreams!

Sustaining of the Will

> [19] Now when his master heard the words of his wife, which she spoke to him, saying, 'This is what your slave did to me,' his anger burned. [20] So Joseph's master took him and put him into the jail, the place where the king's prisoners were confined; and he was there in the jail. [21] But the LORD was with Joseph and extended kindness to him, and gave him favor in the sight of the chief jailer. [22] The chief jailer committed to Joseph's charge all the prisoners who were in the jail; so that whatever was done there, he was responsible *for it*. [23] The chief jailer did not supervise anything under Joseph's charge because the LORD was with him; and whatever he did, the LORD made to prosper.

We close this episode with more signs of God's activity in Joseph's life. The Lord was with Joseph back in Canaan. The Lord stayed by Joseph as a slave in Potiphar's house. And now the Lord shows Himself to be with Joseph as an inmate in Pharaoh's prison.

The chapter begins with God's blessing on Joseph and ends with the same.

Joseph would need that encouragement. Human beings have an incredible will to survive. However, after the treatment Joseph received, he needed the will to be faithful. God's blessing on him in jail strengthened him to be faithful in another unwanted circumstance. More than encouragement arises in the next account. Another divine "coincidence" takes place. The jail Joseph occupies happens to be the very jail where the king's prisoners are detained. That detail proves significant as Joseph does time behind bars.

Chapter 2 – Study/Discussion Questions:

1. Would those who know you say you have a teachable spirit, why or why not?
2. What do you make of the fact that a Christian can make progress in one area, while being blind to flaws in another area of life?
3. How safe do you feel admitting your faults to God?
4. Have you given into temptation recently and not confessed it? Would you take some time to talk with God about it? Review 1 John 1:9.
5. What, if any, painful events have hardened your heart? What do you need to do about it?

Chapter 3

Expensive Clothes Become Affordable When Someone Else Pays for Them
Genesis 40-41

> "... when he had shaved himself and changed his clothes, he came to Pharaoh ... Then Pharaoh took off his signet ring from his hand and put it on Joseph's hand, and clothed him in garments of fine linen and put the gold necklace around his neck" (Genesis 41:15, 42).

I've been known to forget a thing or two, especially during times of stress. Once, while under a heavy load of care, I headed out to run an errand. I got in my car and pushed the remote button to close the garage door. After mashing the button several times without the desired effect, I realized I was pressing a button on our *television* remote. That I carried the TV remote outside in the first place still mystifies me.

On another occasion, I drove up to a gas pump and went inside to pay before pumping. I paid, went back to my car and promptly drove off forgetting to put gas in my tank! I realized my mistake as I got on the ramp to the highway. I went about a quarter mile, to the next exit, and returned to the gas station, and the very same pump. No one had used it in my absence and it was still programed to dispense the gas I had paid for. I immediately began filling my tank without appearing to have paid first. Others filling their cars watched and by the looks on their faces it was obvious they were wondering; "How did you do that?" To be honest, I was wondering; how *could* I do that!

In the next episode of Joseph's life we learn that confinement accelerates a kind of *helpful* forgetting. Yes, occasionally being forgetful comes in handy. In fact, finding God's purpose for our lives sometimes *requires* forgetfulness. Joseph, locked away in jail, has to forget his career plans, his former success in Potiphar's house, and, perhaps, his precious dreams. He must forget *himself* in a way, leaving behind the self-importance we see in earlier episodes of his life. Only then does God promote him.

Confinement can take many forms. One person feels confined in school. Another person suffocates in a claustrophobic relationship. Someone else grates against a job they hate. I languished in an unhealthy family, one that gave me first hand exposure to mental illness.

Growing up with a mother who spent most days lying in bed, staring at the ceiling, and smoking one cigarette after another felt super confining. Watching her get handcuffed, visiting her in mental institutions, and bawling as she put all our furniture on the sidewalk, free for the taking, was like living in an Alfred Hitchcock film. If only it had been a movie instead of real life.

Once, in a break with reality, she made my brothers and I sleep in the backyard, no tent, with just a mattress on the ground.

In her paranoia she felt sure someone would kill us if we slept in the house. That night, she came outside with a long kitchen knife in her hand for "protection." I thought it was probably the last night of my life on earth. I went to sleep convinced I would die at the hands of my own mother.

My mom's problems ran deep, anchored in bitterness and resentment. She never released her pain and madness stalked her. Dulled by chemical balance medication and electric shock treatments, she lived a shell of a woman. We lived together in a straightjacket of a family. What dreams could ever take root in my heart?

Joseph's story teaches us that while we may be at our wits end, our story need not be. If you feel confined by circumstances that lock you into a seemingly nightmarish situation, there is more to your story. You may not be able to imagine it now, but a divine Presence watches over you just as it watched over Joseph. Can you dare to believe it? Once God frees you from your current confines a new day *will* dawn, just as it eventually does for Joseph.

During this era of Joseph's life, locked away in Potiphar's jail, we continue to see him leave clothing behind. In this chapter we'll explore two more references to clothing. The first, Genesis 41:15, appears ever so briefly, yet we dare not miss its significance. In the second reference, Genesis 41:42, we watch someone put clothing *on* Joseph. This second account, where Pharaoh places royal garments on Joseph, shows Joseph finally finding the unique role that God had planned for his life.

Joseph could only wear the robe Pharaoh gave him because his heart was in the right place. In order for our hearts to be in the place God wants, it often involves forgetting imagined outcomes for our lives, our agenda and our plans. Then God can promote us to the next step in *His* plan. Learning to forget one's self, like Joseph does while confined, builds a bridge between the dreams God gives and their fulfillment.

Prison Time

In prison, Joseph begins to experience the same success as in Potiphar's house. He proves such a good administrator that before long he runs the king's prison! Potiphar still trusts Joseph enough to keep him in charge. When two of the king's servants are placed in the jail, *Potiphar* makes sure Joseph takes care of them.[13]

Pharaoh's servants are no ordinary inmates. These men serve the king directly. One morning both men brooded over troubling dreams. Dreams were held to have great significance in that day. These men's dreams were especially so. Joseph asks both men to tell him their dreams. He interprets the first dream as having a positive outcome. Joseph interprets the second dream as having a negative outcome. Both come true as Joseph interprets them. Joseph asks one of the servants, the chief cupbearer, to remember him when he regains his position and help get him out of prison. However, a "slight" delay shows up in a pivotal portion of God's word.

---

[13] Genesis 40:3-4; 39:1

God's Timing Trumps Man's Forgetfulness

> ²³ Yet the chief cupbearer did not remember Joseph, but forgot him. ¹ Now it happened at the end of two full years that Pharaoh had a dream . . . (Genesis 40:23-41:1)

Joseph does his part. He uses his gift of dream interpretation. The dreams of the chief baker and cupbearer work out just as he predicts. The cupbearer goes back to serving Pharaoh, while the chief baker gets his eyes pecked out by vultures.

Despite how things turned out for the baker, Joseph must be encouraged that God used him to interpret these two men's dreams. He must have wondered how long it would take the grateful cupbearer to pull strings and get him out of jail. Will it be a week, a month? Unfortunately for Joseph, *two years* pass between the last verse of Genesis 40 and the opening verse of Genesis 41.

Joseph gets betrayed by his brothers, left to languish in jail by Potiphar and now his one hope, the cupbearer's influence, begins to fade. I want to suggest to you that more than one person's forgetfulness keeps Joseph in jail. God's timing awaits fulfilment.

The time must come for Pharaoh to be ready to let Joseph out of prison. To do so he needs a dream of his own so he can call upon Joseph to interpret it. Pharaoh must have *his* dream! Pharaoh's dream triggers the next step in Joseph's life. It's not all about Joseph. Things have to take place; circumstances have to be set up. Joseph has to trust God while it seems nothing in his life changes.

When God gives you a sense of His purpose for your life and it seems as if nothing changes, hang on! If for no other reason than to demonstrate your faithfulness, hang on. When it seems bad things are happening, don't give up. When it seems as if you're going backwards, God may actually be moving you forward!

There have been a chain of providential events in Joseph's history; being born later in Jacob's life, receiving a controversial gift, meeting a helpful stranger, a timely caravan, slavery in the home of an influential Egyptian, and being forgotten in prison, *Pharaoh's prison*. All this heads toward a predetermined outcome, overseen by a good God.

There will be a chain of providential occurrences in your life too. It may seem you've been opposed, shipped off, harassed, and forgotten. More goes on than you realize. God still remembers you. The circumstances you face stretch your faith to the limit, test your heart to the max, hone your skills, and develop your gifts, just as Joseph's gift of administration soared after arriving in Egypt. The unique circumstances you face may make little sense at times, but God sees things differently.

When the clock of God's timing reaches the hour of your destined purpose it will do so regardless of who has neglected you along the way. Regardless of where you think you should be, looking back, it will make perfect, complete, indisputable sense. God's timing trumps man's forgetfulness.

Self-Forgetfulness Foreshadows Divine Usability

> [14] "Only keep me in mind when it goes well with you, and please do me a kindness by mentioning me to Pharaoh and get me out of this house. [15] For I was in fact kidnapped from the land of the Hebrews, and even here I have done nothing that they should have put me into the dungeon" (Genesis 40:14-16).

Joseph encountered two people who could get him out of prison. First, he pleads his case before the chief cupbearer. Joseph believes that the cupbearer will shortly be released. Anticipating the official's reinstatement, Joseph asks a favor. But what do we discern about Joseph's heart when he asks this favor? He says, "please do me a kindness by mentioning me to Pharaoh." Why would anyone mention a Hebrew slave to the most powerful man on earth? Is that realistic? Does he believe he is worth mentioning to Pharaoh? It seems Joseph wrestles with self-pity and the old strain of self-importance even as God uses him to interpret a dream. This same sentiment surfaced earlier in his life with his brothers and while in Potiphar's service when he says "There is no one greater in this house than I."

Perhaps he simply feels desperate, but a defensive tone echoes from his cell. In Genesis 40:15 Joseph says, "For I was in fact kidnapped from the land of the Hebrews, and even here I have done nothing that they should have put me into the dungeon." Is Joseph completely honest? Was he really kidnapped, as he says? No, he was sold into Egypt by his siblings. Do you get the impression Joseph recognizes God's hand in his situation? Does he grasp what God seeks to do through the troubles he faced? Do you not get the impression he seeks the first possible escape? What if he did get out of jail? Would he not have run home to his father, leaving Egypt and missing God's plan for his life?

I think if we were in Joseph's shoes and saw a chance to get out of jail, we'd go for it. The difficulty arises when Joseph confuses the apparent opportunity to get out of jail and the larger purposes of God. His gift of dream interpretation helps him discern the future, but understanding his present proves more difficult. His inward resistance to his situation causes him to lean toward the expedient, as it would any of us. He just wants to get out of his circumstances.

Compare that scene with his conversation with someone else who could get him out of jail, Pharaoh:

> [14] Then Pharaoh sent and called for Joseph, and they hurriedly brought him out of the dungeon; and when he had shaved himself and changed his clothes, he came to Pharaoh. [15] Pharaoh said to Joseph, "I have had a dream, but no one can interpret it; and I have heard it said about you, that when you hear a dream you can interpret it." [16] Joseph then answered Pharaoh, saying, "It is not in me; God will give Pharaoh a favorable answer" (Genesis 41:14-16).

Joseph has every opportunity to make his case before Pharaoh. Before him lies the perfect opening to act in self-interest. If he ever wanted to advocate for himself, this was his chance. Pharaoh was the man who could remedy the wrongs done to him. But what does he say? "It is not in me; God will give Pharaoh a favorable answer." That's it. He seeks no credit. He asks no favors. He takes no opportunity to petition the king for release. During his entire interview with the king, Joseph demonstrates absolutely no self-interest.

Something Happened in Joseph's Heart

I want to suggest that somewhere between his conversation with the cupbearer and his meeting with the king, two years later, Joseph forgot *himself*. He quit justifying himself to others. He gave up making sense of his life. He was done forcing the issue. He accepted his circumstances. It was all about God now. Whether he ever got out of prison no longer mattered. It now centered on what God wanted and being at peace with it.

Perhaps the dreams of the cupbearer and baker reminded Joseph of his own from a decade earlier. The fulfillment of the two official's dreams might help Joseph see that God was the one who would fulfill his dreams. When the time came, he wouldn't have to lift a finger; God, not Joseph would open the door.

Until we get to this place of self-forgetting, trusting God completely, the Lord cannot move us to the next place in His plan for us. Until we surrender to what He wants to do in our lives, even if we do not like what He does, He cannot move us to the next stage. We too must arrive at the attitude where we say, "It is not in me." Like all of us, Joseph needed to be broken of his self-will and self-importance. During the two additional years he spent in prison that seems to be just what happened.

We get a glimpse into Joseph's heart, during his prison years, in an obscure reference to his life in Psalm 105:17-21:

> He sent a man before them, Joseph, who was sold as a slave. They afflicted his feet with fetters, he himself was laid in irons; until the time that his word came to pass, the word of the LORD tested him. The king sent and released him, the ruler of peoples, and set him free. He made him lord of his house and ruler over all his possessions . . .

David, inspired by the Holy Spirit, introduces us to an aspect of Joseph's ordeal that other sources don't mention. The brutal reality of slavery and prison life, while not highlighted by Moses' record, gets special attention from David's pen. Joseph's incarceration was no minimum security life of luxury, "they afflicted his feet with fetters, he himself was laid in irons."

While in irons, "the word of the LORD tested him." Joseph was tested while he waited for God to fulfill his promise. That much is obvious. However the testing was more than that. God uses the pit, slavery, and prison to prepare his heart for his dream's fulfillment. The irons that entered Joseph's life reached into his very soul. His incarceration weakened the self-importance that trailed him from his youth. Joseph passes the hard test every believer must face, being broken of self-rule.

The process of being broken and yielding to God flies in the face of human nature. It's a lesson some of God's people learn faster than others. Some believers never learn it. Until we do, we likely face what Joseph faced, cycles of painful discipline set in place by a divine Hand. God loves us enough to make us confront ourselves through the various difficulties we encounter in life. He allows painful crises to test us, to break us. The question remains; are we discerning and learning the lessons He intends?

Paul Billhiemer in his book, *Don't Waste Your Sorrows*, writes, "One is not broken until all resentment and rebellion against God and man is removed, one who resents, takes offense, or retaliates against criticism and oppression or lack of appreciation is unbroken. All self-justification and irritation with providential circumstances and situations reveals un-brokenness. Genuine brokenness usually requires years of crushing heartache and sorrow. Thus are self-will surrendered and deep degrees of yieldedness and submission developed."[14] The work of surrender God needed to do in Joseph, God also works in us.

Could you have done what Joseph did when he stood before Pharaoh? Could you face the opportunity to get out of a situation you hate and not pull strings? Could you resist the chance to free yourself from difficulty, deferring to God's wisdom? God cannot trust us with the next step in His plan if we try to take that next step on our own. Let's see what happens when Joseph allows God to do it His way.

Forgotten Prosperity Stirs a King's Will

> [29] Behold, seven years of great abundance are coming in all the land of Egypt; [30] and after them seven years of famine will come, and all the abundance will be forgotten in the land of Egypt, and the famine will ravage the land. [31] So the abundance will be unknown in the land because of that subsequent famine;

---

[14] Paul E. Billheimer, *Don't Waste Your Sorrows* (Christian Literature Crusade: Fort Washington PA 1977) 75.

for it *will be* very severe. ³² Now as for the repeating of the dream to Pharaoh twice, *it means* that the matter is determined by God, and God will quickly bring it about. ³³ Now let Pharaoh look for a man discerning and wise, and set him over the land of Egypt. ³⁴ Let Pharaoh take action to appoint overseers in charge of the land, and let him exact a fifth *of the produce* of the land of Egypt in the seven years of abundance. ³⁵ Then let them gather all the food of these good years that are coming, and store up the grain for food in the cities under Pharaoh's authority, and let them guard *it*. ³⁶ Let the food become as a reserve for the land for the seven years of famine which will occur in the land of Egypt, so that the land will not perish during the famine." ³⁷ Now the proposal seemed good to Pharaoh and to all his servants (Genesis 41:29-37).

To advance in God's plan, Pharaoh must appoint Joseph prime minister of Egypt. What would motivate a king, to elevate a state prisoner to the second highest post in the land? What would motivate one of the Pharaohs, with all we know about that dynasty, to promote a foreigner, let alone one who was a slave, to be his right hand man? Yet God prearranges circumstances so that Pharaoh *willingly* promotes Joseph.

It comes together like clockwork. First, the king dreams about livestock and harvest. The dreams so trouble him that he anxiously considers their meaning. Secondly, none of his usual advisers are capable of interpreting the dreams. Thirdly, the cupbearer, who, for fear of reminding the king about his previous offenses, who never brought Joseph up in conversation, does so now. Now it appears safe and helpful to do so because the matter proves urgent and relevant. God makes Joseph, an unknown, obscure slave relevant to Pharaoh! In a matter of minutes Joseph gets ushered out of prison and into Pharaoh's presence. What a shock when the notice came to hurry up and send Joseph to the king!

Notice a little phase easy to overlook, ". . . when he had shaved himself and *changed his clothes*, he came to Pharaoh" (Italics mine). Again Joseph leaves clothing behind, representing a deep and final change of heart in this man. We know it is permanent because he never goes back again to any kind of confinement or cycles of pain.

Joseph's most recent change of clothes models a change in his heart; a fashion statement of a self-life left behind. His new clothes gained him entry to the next stage of his life. Sometimes we're not dressed right for the occasions God has in mind. If we advance to the next step in God's plan wearing our old clothes, we will not fit in. We will look out of place. Not Joseph, his old clothing no longer fits and he leaves his prison garb behind.

When Pharaoh meets Joseph he explains his dreams and Joseph interprets them. What a scene. The most powerful man in the known world unveiling his heart to a prison convict. Joseph gives the explanation; after seven years of abundance will come seven years of famine, "and the abundance will become forgotten in the land of Egypt; and the famine will ravage the land." Pharaoh dreamt a good news – bad news dream. Seven years of abundance lay on the horizon, with seven more years of famine just beyond. The abundance will be forgotten by the severity of the famine.

What would motivate the most powerful man in the world to

promote one of the least powerful men in the world? The threat of economic disaster! Joseph's interpretation resonates with certitude. His plan to store the surplus of the first seven years to cover the lack of the second makes immediate sense to Pharaoh.

It takes the concern of a king to motivate a king. What concerns a king? Is he concerned about the things you and I are concerned about? No, he worries about his power, his reign, and his legacy. When such a man hears that economic disaster will occur on his watch, he becomes open to solutions. The threat of forgotten abundance motivated the most powerful man in the world to cooperate with God's plan.

> [41] Pharaoh said to Joseph, "See, I have set you over all the land of Egypt." [42]Then Pharaoh took off his signet ring from his hand and put it on Joseph's hand, and clothed him in garments of fine linen and put the gold necklace around his neck (Genesis 41:41-42).

Here we see someone putting clothes *on* Joseph rather than trying to take them off. The coat his brothers ripped and the cloak Potiphar's wife stripped both represented place and standing. The clothing Pharaoh places on Joseph represents the very same things! So what's different? The symbolism of the clothing remains the same, but the person wearing the clothing has changed. Joseph finally walks down the fashion runway of life worthy of his clothing.

The prison clothes he wore a few minutes earlier will never be put on again. Joseph makes a break with his painful past. He steps into the outfit God designed for him thirteen years earlier. It's happening. It's really happening! Getting new clothes, like a fresh start, brings hope into Joseph's life – especially when the King buys your clothes.

I can't help but snicker as I imagine what Mrs. Potiphar thought when she got the news. I would have loved to see the look on her lying face. The slave she framed for attempted rape now ruled the land, second only to Pharaoh. Ha! She probably packed her bags and booked a long trip down the Nile, never to return.

When It's Your Turn

When the time comes to fulfill your role in God's plan, it may not be a Pharaoh you stand before. It may not be a king who holds sway over your life. It may be an employer. It may be a parent. It may be your need to finish school. At times, it may seem like people, or things, hold you back. When your time comes, God will move in that person's heart, doors *will* open. It may seem impossible to believe that the authority figure looming over you wants to do anything in your favor. But God has His ways and they often surprise us. At the right time, He moves the hearts of men to accomplish His purposes. In the meantime, you may have to get comfortable in the shadows of life. Can you wait until God knows you are ready? Can you trust Him? Can you hold on until God moves in the heart of the one who holds sway over your life?

Fruitfulness & Forgetting

> [50] Now before the year of famine came, two sons were born to Joseph, whom Asenath, the daughter of Potiphera priest of On, bore to him. [51] Joseph named the firstborn Manasseh, "For," *he said*, "God has made me forget all my trouble and all my father's household." [52] He named the second Ephraim, "For," *he said*, "God has made me fruitful in the land of my affliction" (Genesis 41:50-52).

We fast forward now. Joseph serves as prime minister and works his NCSP (National Crop Storage Program). Pharaoh gives him a wife. She gives birth to two sons and Joseph names them. The first he names Manasseh, which means "making to forget." Joseph's new life in Egypt enabled him to forget his former hardships. The second son he names Ephraim, which means "fruitfulness." By assigning this name, Joseph means to say, "God has made me fruitful in the land of my affliction." With the naming of His two sons, he begins to make sense of his life. He can finally sit down and reflect upon the path God placed him. He sees God's hand implementing a perfect and amazing plan. Joseph faced painful episodes, but now the fruitfulness of the present (Ephraim) helps him forget (Manasseh) the pain of the past.

Joseph finds a measure of healing in his sons. Wrenched from his family, the separation took its toll. Ten years as a slave left its mark. His years in prison? Tormenting. His young adult life consisted of repeated cycles of painful experiences. Joseph needed healing because his story is not over. A larger narrative is yet to play out.

God has plans to raise up a nation for Himself and Joseph prepares the way. Joseph's part in the plan goes back to God's covenant with Abraham, "And God said to Abram, 'Know for certain that your descendants will be strangers in a land that is not theirs, where they will be enslaved and oppressed four hundred years. But I will also judge the nation whom they will serve; and afterward they will come out with many possessions.'"[15]

Did Joseph know that he would lead the Israelites into that promise? I doubt it, at least not at this point. Later, when his brothers and father move to Egypt, he knows. Joseph says in Genesis 50:24, "I am about to die, but God will surely take care of you, and bring you up from this land to the land which He promised on oath to Abraham, Isaac and to Jacob."

Summary

Locked in Pharaoh's dungeon, Joseph learns a freeing lesson. In the darkest hours of his life he vainly waits for the king's cupbearer to get him out of jail. While he waits, he confronts the dimly lit corners of his heart. He could not deny the evidence of God's favor, wherever his abusers sent him, but something kept tripping him up. What was it? Suddenly, in the sunshine of an unrecorded day, Joseph yields his dreams, his future, and his station in life to God. Free from the need to impress, he waits contentedly in prison for God to do whatever God would do. Joseph forgets himself.

---

[15] Genesis 15:13-14

Then the chief cupbearer finally remembers him. When the king has a dream he can't shake, Joseph gives Pharaoh an unforgettable interpretation. Then, Joseph experiences the unimaginable. He becomes second in command of all Egypt! As he begins his new role, Joseph finds healing from the pain that brought him there in the first place. Finding healing from deep hurt and discovering one's role in God's plan flowed from forgetting himself.

Would you ask God to bring you to the place of self-forgetting? Would you ask Him to help you admit, like Joseph, "It is not in me"? In our day, dominated by self-reliance, such a confession seems outmoded. If you've been deeply wounded, letting your guard down can be especially hard, admitting you don't have all the answers. You may not have the answers for the pain you've experienced, but God does.

Once again we see a change of clothing. Pharaoh bought new clothes for Joseph because he was the kind of person Pharaoh could use. God wants to broaden your range of usefulness too, making you worthy of new clothes and the fresh outlook that comes with them. It begins by yielding your pain and your self-rule to God.

Chapter 3 – Study/Discussion Questions:

1. Have you ever tried to get yourself out of circumstances you did not like, but God kept you there? What do you think God was trying to do in your life at the time?
2. Do you believe God is able to work out His plan for your life even when you do not see how? What scriptures might encourage you along these lines?
3. How does forgetting oneself relate to God's ability to use you?
4. In what ways does God's blessing in the present help heal us from hurts in the past? Can you site a personal example?
5. Joseph wrestled with his painful history. What is one thing from the past with which you struggle?

JOSEPH UNROBED

Chapter 4

Disguises Sometimes Come in Handy
Genesis 42

"When Joseph saw his brothers he recognized them, but he disguised himself to them" (Genesis 42:7).

The letter I pulled from my college mailbox made me curious. The return address looked unfamiliar. When I opened the envelope I was dumbfounded. It was from my dad. What was it? Twelve or thirteen years since he left? I couldn't remember. No one had been able to find him. He never paid child support. He was a wanted man because of it. Whatever his reason for writing, I couldn't help but notice he had beautiful handwriting. It unsettled me. How could this paternal stranger who had crushed me have beautiful handwriting? I never imagined he might possess a *good* quality. Questions raced through my mind, "How did he know where to find me?" "What did he want?" As I pondered why he wrote, I felt my insides coming unglued.

I read the letter. He wanted to get to know me. He wanted to be in my life. He asked, "Would I send him a picture?" I struggled. I knew that as a Christian I bore an obligation to forgive him. While I no longer desired to get even, I could barely restrain the involuntary desire to lash out. I may have forgiven him in my head, but my heart never got the message. Too many emotions were stored up, yet to be vented.

I wrote back. I sent a picture. I tried to act Christian. Yet when his second letter arrived, it contained a condition for moving forward. He explained that to have a relationship with him, I would have to completely forget everything that happened (or didn't happen) before. I tried to hide my grief. His second letter revealed no real sorrow over his actions. He wanted the benefits of a relationship without taking responsibility for the past. He had never faced the reality of what he had done. Though I had lived with the pain since the day he left. What could I do? I wrote back and explained I would not accept the condition he set. I couldn't disguise my feelings about the pain he caused me.

At least I got a letter and not an unexpected visit. But Joseph's bothers show back up in his life, *in person!* I imagine it sent a jolt through his system. What would he do? We learn that Joseph disguises himself and his feelings, for a time. The man we've seen change his clothes more than once, does it again. We don't know if his disguise included an actual change of clothes, but he altered his appearance in a manner that left his brothers clueless to his true identity.

The story shifts focus here on at least two levels. First, it turns out that Joseph is not the only one wearing a disguise. His brothers wear them too. They live a double life, guilty of betrayal, all the while putting forth a false image of honesty. They may have disguised their sin, but they cannot escape the psychological impact of what they did to Joseph twenty years earlier. Their masquerade of innocence affects the way they relate with each other and their father. However, the unmasking of their guilt, in this episode, sets them up for reconciliation later in the story.

Secondly, previous episodes of Joseph's life contained large doses of personal pain. The pain of those earlier times anticipates the pain we see him experience now. For just as the pain of breaking a bone precedes the pain of resetting that same bone, we watch as Joseph works to reset his broken relationship with his extended family. And it is *painful*. As painful as it might be, reconciliation with his family was part of God's larger plan for Israel.

These changes in focus have relational healing in view. For healing to occur, Joseph's brothers must face their past. Their awkward first meeting sets the stage for a touching reunion story that unfolds later. But first, the brothers must deal with themselves as they once sought to deal with "this dreamer," their brother Joseph. The following scene provides an epic lesson on the nature of suppressed guilt and how God uses it to restore the relationship between Joseph and his brothers.

The Suppression of Guilt

> [1] Now Jacob saw that there was grain in Egypt, and Jacob said to his sons, 'Why are you staring at one another?' [2] He said, 'Behold, I have heard that there is grain in Egypt; go down there and buy *some* for us from that place, so that we may live and not die.' [3] Then ten brothers of Joseph went down

> to buy grain from Egypt. ⁴ But Jacob did not send Joseph's brother Benjamin with his brothers, for he said, 'I am afraid that harm may befall him.'⁵ So the sons of Israel came to buy grain among those who were coming, for the famine was in the land of Canaan *also* (Genesis 42:1-5).

The famine which motivated Pharaoh to promote Joseph now motivates Jacob to send his ten sons to Egypt to buy grain. The famine's regional impact reaches all the way to Canaan, but the story opens with a strange question. "Jacob said to his sons, 'Why are you staring at one another?'" Jacob's sons likely knew there was grain in Egypt, but something inside them resists going there. Could it be that the thought of Egypt troubles their minds? The Bible suggests they knew the Ishmaelite traders, to whom they sold Joseph, were headed for Egypt.[16] Every time Egypt came up in conversation it reminded them of their crime. Hesitating for reasons they dare not disclose, they stumble over their suppressed guilt. Joseph's brothers hem and haw to their father's consternation. If Jacob only knew why they were staring at each other!

Humans struggle to suppress guilt. It might be a word, a look, or even awkward silence, but eventually the guilt is exposed. Sometimes suppressed guilt takes the form of irritability, certain topics that get ruled off limits, or a lapse of relational spontaneity. Interpersonal communication gets hamstrung, every word guarded, every thought edited, lest the truth accidentally comes to light. So, imagine ten brothers trying to keep a secret from their wives,

---

[16] Genesis 37:25-28; 45:4-5

children, and father for *twenty years*. The odds of them keeping a lid on what they did to Joseph are astronomical.

Every year at Joseph's birthday or the anniversary of his disappearance, the brothers would have to keep quiet. Each time a memento of Joseph's surfaces, they are reminded of what they had done. When Jacob grieves over the loss of Joseph, they fake sympathy. One action twenty years earlier distorts the culture of the entire clan. They must suppress what they know they did together. What a burden.

Parents have radar for inconsistencies in manner that betray guilty behavior by their kids. Jacob was no different. That "Jacob did not send Joseph's brother Benjamin with his brothers" may suggest a degree of mistrust in the family. Jacob's loss of Joseph puts fear in his heart regarding Benjamin, "for he said, 'I am afraid that harm may befall him." Jacob's sons were known to cause harm. They had a history of deception and violence. When they took vengeance on Shechem, for the abuse of their sister Dinah, Jacob commented, "You have brought trouble on me, by making me odious among the inhabitants of the land."[17]

At times in his life Jacob appears to be a fearful man, but in this case his fears were justified. He felt the sons of Rachel did not fare well in the company of their brothers. Something inside Jacob told him not to let Benjamin go to Egypt. His unwillingness sent a message that his other sons no doubt picked up. This too reawakened their individual and collective guilt.

---

[17] Genesis 34:30

When the brothers finally arrive in Egypt they kneel before Joseph, dramatically fulfilling his earlier dreams. Joseph recognizes them immediately. He disguises himself and accuses them of being spies. His brothers vigorously protested and declare that they are honest men! Yet, in the next breath, they lie about what happened to Joseph years ago, describing him as "no longer being alive."[18] How can a party proclaim their honesty and be guilty at the same time? Could it be they've told the story of Joseph's death for so long that they've come to believe it? Perhaps, but, as Joseph accuses them of espionage, suppressed guilt quickly rises to their consciousness.

The Associations of Guilt

> [18] Now Joseph said to them on the third day, "Do this and live, for I fear God: [19] if you are honest men, let one of your brothers be confined in your prison; but as for *the rest of* you, go, carry grain for the famine of your households, [20] and bring your youngest brother to me, so your words may be verified, and you will not die." And they did so. [21] Then they said to one another, "Truly we are guilty concerning our brother, because we saw the distress of his soul when he pleaded with us, yet we would not listen; therefore this distress has come upon us." [22] Reuben answered them, saying, "Did I not tell you, 'Do not sin against the boy'; and you would not listen? Now comes the reckoning for his blood." [23] They did not know, however, that Joseph understood, for there was an interpreter between them (Genesis 42:18-23).

---

[18] Genesis 42:13

Joseph's test of their motives for coming to Egypt immediately brings his brothers' guilt to the surface. They openly discuss their sin, thinking Joseph cannot understand them. They interpret the trouble coming upon them as recompense for the trouble they caused Joseph. The immediate association of their current trouble with their twenty year old guilt is astounding. They discuss it as if their crime occurred two weeks previous! What they did to Joseph no doubt feels recent because they failed to escape their guilty feelings over the years. Their guilt troubles them to the point they pay no attention to the first of several clues Joseph drops about his true identity. Note that Joseph says, "Do this and live for I fear God." Why would an Egyptian official have any interest in gods other than those found in Egypt? Nevertheless, Joseph's remark goes right over his brothers' heads.

The brother's *collective* assent to the punitive nature of their current dilemma is fascinating. That "They said to one another, 'Truly we are guilty concerning our brother'" reveals a *consensus* of feeling as to their ill-treatment by Pharaoh's official. They, themselves, provide confirmation, recognition, of divine discipline upon their lives for what they had done.

What led them to connect their past treatment of Joseph with their current predicament?

- The brothers were all together, just as they had been twenty years earlier when they disposed of Joseph.
- Their father was absent. They were free to discuss the matter among themselves.

- Benjamin stayed home. Had he been allowed to accompany his brothers to Egypt, their conversation could not flow openly. Something might get back to Jacob.
- With every step they took toward Egypt they relived their actions. They were headed to the very place where they sold their brother.
- When they arrive in Egypt, they receive harsh treatment. In spite of their pleas, the prince of the land refuses to heed their claims of innocence. The treatment they receive triggers a recollection of the treatment they doled out to Joseph, two decades earlier.

When we feel guilty, and seek to repress it, anything or anyone associated with our guilt reminds us of our offense. Even if we succeed in consciously suppressing our guilt during the day, it often enters our dreams at night. Seneca wrote, "Every guilty person is his own hangman." We may escape the law, but the law never escapes us.

Joseph's brothers squirm before Joseph. Rueben, the eldest but not the wisest, begins to point fingers. In verse twenty-two he says, "Did I not tell you, 'Do not sin against the boy; and you would not listen? Now comes the reckoning for his blood.'" One wonders if Rueben knew what really happened to Joseph. With the reference to Joseph's "blood" he may have assumed his brothers killed him. Rueben seems to be off scene when Joseph gets sold to the Ishmaelites as his reaction to Joseph's absence from the pit suggests.[19] If so, there were secrets within secrets, some brothers knew more than others. Rueben, trying to make up for mistakes of his youth, never seems to regain the respect of his brothers or his father.[20] The other brothers may have decided he could not be trusted to keep the facts of the matter to himself.

The Anxieties of Guilt

> [25] Then Joseph gave orders to fill their bags with grain and to restore every man's money in his sack, and to give them provisions for the journey. And thus it was done for them. [26] So they loaded their donkeys with their grain and departed from there. [27] As one *of them* opened his sack to give his donkey fodder at the lodging place, he saw his money; and behold, it was in the mouth of his sack. [28] Then he said to his brothers, "My money has been returned, and behold, it is even in my sack." And their hearts sank, and they *turned* trembling to one another, saying, "What is this that God has done to us?"
>
> [35] Now it came about as they were emptying their sacks, that behold, every man's bundle of money *was* in his sack; and when they and their father saw their bundles of money, they were dismayed (Genesis 42:25-28; 35).

After three days, Joseph decides to keep one of his brothers locked up so the others can return home with food for their families. He selects Simeon to remain in Egypt under lock and key. Joseph conditions his release upon the nine returning to Egypt with Benjamin, their youngest brother, to prove their innocence from the spying charges. Joseph knows the famine has just begun and his brothers will need to return for more grain. His brothers cannot escape their ancient wrongdoing, but a sense of relief, no doubt,

---

[19] Genesis 37:29-30
[20] Genesis 35:22; 42:37-38; 49:3-4

settles over them as they head home.

It doesn't last long. When they stop for the night, an unnamed brother opens a sack of grain to feed his donkey and discovers the money he used to pay for his grain! His reaction, as well as that of his brothers', demonstrates the high degree of anxiety often associated with guilt.

Upon discovery of the money, notice what they do not say. They don't say, "Uh-oh, somebody made a mistake." Neither does the one who found the money exclaim, "Woo hoo, I won the lottery, look boys found money!" No one congratulates him and says, "Dang, you are always so lucky!" They could have said, "That Egyptian official sure is generous!" But they do not. Their response to the discovery of money in the sack reflects nothing an innocent person might say.

Instead, the Bible says, "Their hearts sank." Why? Why would they assume the worst? Because guilt and anxiety walk hand in hand. The brothers becomes so anxious, imagine this now, they all began to *tremble*. These rough and ready shepherds, men prone to violence - never backing down from a fight, begin to physically *tremble*. By what they say next you'd think they were all good Calvinists, "What is this that *God* has done to us?" (Italics mine)

What *is* God doing to them? He applies pressure to break them. He corners them to lead them to repentance. These men threw their brother in a pit then casually sat down to eat a meal (Genesis 37:25). They considered murdering Joseph, but at the last minute shipped him off. Consumed by malice they willing broke their father's heart with a lie. They now stand trembling, weak at the knees, bearing the full force of two decades worth of anxiety.

The brothers trudge home and open their sacks. Each discovers the money meant to purchase grain. How did they respond? ". . . when they and their father saw their bundles of money, they were dismayed." The situation exceeded their ability to grasp it. Even Jacob was thrown off course. It might all seem like a bad dream except for the absence of Simeon. He waited behind in an Egyptian jail.

If Jacob had his wits about him, he would have asked his sons, "If the Egyptian official gave you such a hard time, why is your money in your sacks?" He could have innocently asked, "What have you boys been up to?" The weight of their feelings would have done them in. They would have spilled all regarding Joseph. Instead, Jacob, consumed by his own grief, thinks only of himself. He says, "You have bereaved me of my children: Joseph is no more, and Simeon is no more, and you would take Benjamin; all these things are against me" (Genesis 42:36). Or, so it seemed. Ironically, all these things are *for* Jacob. He just failed to see beyond his apparent loses. God would use each imagined loss to bring great gains to many.

Sleepless Nights

Imagine the brothers' anxiety as a second trip to Egypt loomed. Such worries lead to sleepless nights. They once caused

Joseph a nightmare of an experience when they sold him off to Egypt. Now, no doubt, they're beginning to have their own! Each trip to Egypt brings reminders of their guilt. God desires to set them free from their guilt and the impact on their families.

He leads them all toward healing. In His amazing kindness, He also leads Joseph's brothers to fulfill *their* roles in His purposes. After what they had done to Joseph, it might seem unsettling to think that God has good in mind for Joseph's brothers. However, God weaves pain and purpose together in Joseph's brothers' lives, just as He does in Joseph's.

The work God is doing in their hearts provides hope for us. If He can work in their hearts, He can work in ours. If He can work in the lives of Joseph's brothers, then He can work in the lives of those who have injured us.

Chapter 4 – Study/Discussion Questions:

1. Have you ever worn a disguise? What was it and what was the occasion?
2. How does the fact that Joseph's brothers sinned as a group, as well as individually, color the situation?
3. What challenges did Joseph's brothers face as they hid their sin for twenty years?
4. How hard is it to confess a sin that has defined you for many years?
5. Is there a sin in your life to which you've become accustomed?

Chapter 5

Returns are Easier if You Have Your Receipt – Genesis 43-44

"Then they tore their clothes, and when each man loaded his donkey, they returned to the city" (Genesis 44:13).

Some thirty years after my father left, I still wrestled with the loss. Watching my own kids grow up in a stable family demonstrated how God had turned my life around. I enjoyed a significant measure of healing through the help of a gifted counselor. Years of journaling helped me vent buried grief and anger. My wise and thoughtful wife often spoke into my pain, reminding me of my value. I found rest in my identity in Christ and His daily presence. Yet, in my late thirties, I still couldn't free myself from the hurt of my father's rejection. Like trying to get free from the arms of a giant octopus, some tentacles resisted removal. Though far less potent, I tired of the pain's presence. Wearied by the battle, I asked the Lord for help.

Imagine my surprise, a few days later, when I walked out to our mailbox and another letter greeted me. Though nearly two decades had passed since the first one, I recognized the beautiful handwriting on the envelope. I immediately knew the letter was from my father. My heart began to race. I didn't open it right away. I wanted to wait till I could get alone. This could be good, or, this could be bad. Since I had prayed for some kind of relief, I felt mild optimism at the letter's arrival. That it showed up at all astonished me.

Like me, Joseph's brothers needed to revisit an old issue. They ran out of grain from their first trip to Egypt. With no other options, hunger forces them to return. Meanwhile, their brother Simeon sits in jail pining for them to reappear. If Simeon had not served as human collateral, and they could have bought grain elsewhere, I doubt they would have returned to face that difficult Egyptian official, their brother Joseph in disguise.

In Genesis 43-44 Joseph's brothers make a nerve wracking return trip to Egypt. I would encourage you to take a moment to read that passage. Few scenes in the Bible provide more drama. As their first supply of grain runs out so did Jacob's reluctance to send Benjamin with them. Finding the money they used to purchase their first load of grain in their sacks causes them no shortage of concern over what awaits them in Egypt. If only they had gotten a receipt to prove they paid for their first shipment. Think what anxieties they could have avoided!

Once the brothers arrive in Egypt they are ushered into Joseph's home. Again, their anxiety leads them to assume the worst. In their paranoia, they believe they face impending enslavement at the hands of this troublesome Egyptian official. The brothers prove so paranoid they worry this Egyptian, with whom they will share a meal, wants their donkeys too! Notice how their apprehension colors the motives they project on their host, "It is because of the money that was returned in our sacks the first time that we are being brought in, that he may seek occasion against us and fall upon us, and take us for slaves with our donkeys" (Genesis 43:18).

God Sets Up the Guilty

Joseph's brothers expect the worst, but they receive surprising news when the house steward discloses that he put the money in their sacks. What must they have thought when the steward tells them, "Be at ease, do not be afraid. 'Your God and the God of your father has given you treasure in your sacks. I had your money'" (Genesis 43: 23). Did his words "Your God and the God of your father" register with them? They are so relieved they fail to question the steward's knowledge of their father's God. They miss another clue to what is really going on.

Joseph, for his part, barely holds it together. The sight of his younger brother Benjamin, moves him deeply, so deeply, he excuses himself to weep. The reunion overwhelms him. Joseph realizes his dreams are fulfilled and God's purposes begin to unfold before his eyes. However he keeps his disguise on a little longer. In the meantime, they share a meal together, sort of. The Egyptian practice of not eating with foreigners provided a convenient way for Joseph to hide his feelings from his brothers, as they ate in separate areas of the house.

What happens next provides Joseph's brothers with more missed clues that something fishy is going on. When they realize the seating arrangement reflects their birth order the Bible reports, "the men looked at one another in astonishment" (Genesis 43:33). And how did they explain the abundance of food given to Benjamin compared to their portions? Somehow they also miss the meaning of Joseph's incessant questions about their father (Genesis 43:7, 27). Joseph gives them clues to his identity which they fail to pick up. Instead, they begin to relax and enjoy lunch. The Bible tells us, "So they feasted and drank freely with him" (Genesis 43:34).

The brothers, relieved about the money discovered in their sacks, believe the issue settled. Free from the spying charge, everything goes well. Even Simeon seems no worse for wear after his time in jail. During the luncheon, the brothers began to think they are off the hook. Facing divine discipline for the distress they caused Joseph now seems like something they imagined. It had all been a bad dream. Everything would be alright now. They could come and go freely and avoid any more reminders of their guilt. Life looked bright again.

Little do they know they are being set up, not only by Joseph but by *God*. You see, for guilty individuals, to deal with their guilt, they must come to the place where they feel safe enough to let their guard down. They cannot resolve guilt and hide guilt at the same time. So, by assuaging their fears, as they do in this scene at the luncheon, the brothers begin to feel better about their situation, forgetting their troubled consciences. Their defenses go down. And as they do, God inches them closer toward admitting their guilt.

As the happy band leaves Joseph's house, they head home loaded with full grain sacks. But they are unaware that both their money and a special cup lay hidden among them. Joseph frames them for something they did not do, so that they can come clean about something they really did. He sends his steward after them and upon catching up with the men, charges them with theft. The brothers are aghast at the accusation and respond with an over the top claim of innocence. "Far be it from your servants to do such a thing . . . with whomever of your servants it is found, let him die, and we also will be my lord's slaves" (Genesis 44:7, 9).

When the cup surfaces in Benjamin's sack, it devastates the entire group. The immediate implications for themselves and for their father hit them full force. In shock and grief they *tear their clothes*. Years ago they tore clothes off their innocent brother, now they tear their own!

They declare their collective guilt, even when it appears perpetrated only by Benjamin. They betrayed Joseph but they stick by Benjamin. My, how things have changed. Their stunning statement carries a veiled double meaning in verses 14-16, "*God has found out the iniquity of your servants;* behold we are my lord's slaves, both we and the one in whose possession the cup has been found" (Italics mine). What sin were they referring to? Was it only the implied guilt of Benjamin or something deeper, the lingering guilt of an ancient offense? It seems that if they could not return to their father with Benjamin, none of them wanted to return at all. When Joseph insists that only Benjamin become his slave, Judah steps up and gives one of the most beautiful recorded speeches in the Bible (Genesis 44:18-34).

God Transforms the Ringleader

> [18] Then Judah approached him, and said, "Oh my lord, may your servant please speak a word in my lord's ears, and do not be angry with your servant; for you are equal to Pharaoh. [19] My lord asked his servants, saying, 'Have you a father or a brother?' [20] We said to my lord, 'We have an old father and a little child of *his* old age. Now his brother is dead, so he alone is left of his mother, and his father loves him.' [21] Then you said to your servants, 'Bring him down to me that I may set my eyes on him.' [22] But we said to my lord, 'The lad cannot leave his father, for if he should leave his father, his father would die.' [23] You said to your servants, however, 'Unless your youngest brother comes down with you, you will not see my face again.' [24] Thus it came about when we went up to your servant my father, we told him the words of my lord. [25] Our father said, 'Go back, buy us a little food.' [26] But we said, 'We cannot go down. If our youngest brother is with us, then we will go down; for we cannot see the man's face unless our youngest brother is with us.' [27] Your servant my father said to us, 'You know that my wife bore me two sons; [28] and the one went out from me, and I said, "Surely he is torn in pieces," and I have not seen him since. [29] If you take this one also from me, and harm befalls him, you will bring my gray hair down to Sheol in sorrow.' [30] Now, therefore, when I come to your servant my father, and the lad is not with us, since his life is bound up in the lad's life, [31] when he sees that the lad is not *with us*, he will die. Thus your servants will bring the gray hair of your servant our father down to Sheol in sorrow. [32] For your servant became surety for the lad to my father, saying, 'If I do not bring him *back* to you, then let me bear the blame before my father forever.' [33] Now,

therefore, please let your servant remain instead of the lad a slave to my lord, and let the lad go up with his brothers. 34 For how shall I go up to my father if the lad is not with me—for fear that I see the evil that would overtake my father?"

This is the second time Judah takes center stage in the Joseph narrative and the contrast between the two is dramatic.[21] Here we have a man desperate to return Benjamin to his father. Judah empathizes with his father's affection for Benjamin and the effect it will have on Jacob if Benjamin remains in Egypt. Judah, tenderhearted and passionate in his plea, selflessly offers to serve as a slave in Benjamin's place. To say Judah's speech touches the heart barely scratches the surface. The speech reveals Judah to be a changed man.

Do you remember whose idea it was to sell Joseph to the Ishmaelite traders in the first place? It was Judah's.[22] Judah led the way in selling Joseph and participated in the earlier retribution doled out on Shechem.[23] His former character also takes center stage in a sordid affair recorded in Genesis 38. That story when compared with the speech he gives before Joseph reveals that, during the intervening years, God worked in Judah as deeply as He had worked in Joseph.

How does God work in the heart of an abuser like Judah? God gives him trouble of his own. God arranges circumstances so that the offender feels the pain of his or her actions. It may take years

---

[21] See Genesis 38
[22] Genesis 37:26-27
[23] Genesis 34

for the damage one causes to dawn on the wrongdoer. Sadly, sometimes it never does, but where the heart contains a glimmer of God's presence such a one may come to his or her senses.

In Judah's case his troubles start with his marriage to a Canaanite woman. He married outside the clan, blending with the culture around him. Three sons are born from the marriage. Two of which go on to commit such evil acts that through divine arrangement they die early deaths. Judah (like his father) experiences all the frustration associated with children who grow into rebels. When his relationships with his sons get cut short by their early demise, he can identify with his father's loss of Joseph and now potentially of Benjamin.

The earlier character of Judah also reveals a man who indulges his passions. He engages in sex with someone he thinks a random prostitute. Only later, Judah discovers he slept with Tamar, his widowed daughter-in-law! Before he realizes that he fathered the child she carries, Judah stands ready to exact the full penalty for her adultery.

God uses Tamar's actions to work in Judah's heart. The tradition of levirate marriage was common in that day. It stipulates that if a husband dies without an heir, a close male relative should produce an heir through the widow. The tradition protects a family line from being extinguished. Judah's first son, Er, married Tamar, but he was so evil the Lord took his life. Judah's second son, Onan, died as the result of divine judgment for his misbehavior in the levirate custom. Judah has no interest in losing a third son through association with Tamar. His reluctance, over the years, to have his son Shelah marry Tamar, motivates Tamar to deceive Judah into impregnating her.

Judah, no stranger to deception or extinguishing a family line (killing the men of Shechem and by selling off Joseph), confesses at the end of the story: "She (Tamar) is more righteous than I."[24] His statement shows Judah thinking in terms of right and wrong. His awakened conscience proves a dangerous precedent for a man guilty of worse sins. The confession of one wrong makes it hard for him to hide from other indictments hidden in his heart. When Judah returns to Egypt for the second trip and the crisis over Benjamin erupts, God has prepared his heart. He easily empathizes with Jacob's potential pain, should he suffer the loss of another favored son. He's been through it himself.

It takes years for Judah's transformation to occur, just as it took years for Joseph's. But this same man, Judah, now utters the amazing words, "Now therefore, please let your servant remain instead of the lad a slave to my lord, and let the lad go up with his brothers."

This man, years ago, thought only of self. Now he thinks of his father and the pain Benjamin's absence would bring him. What tenderness took root in Judah's heart? How did this man go from being a sibling nemesis to a sibling protector? The grace of God knows no depths. The work God wrought in Judah's heart was such that the Lion of Judah, the Messiah, arises from his family's

---

[24] Genesis 38:26

line. The substitutionary solution Judah offers Joseph, to save Benjamin from slavery and his father from grief, bears the same character as Christ's work on the cross for those whose place He came to take.

God Transforms Another

My shock resembled Joseph's, at seeing his brothers, when, in my late thirties, I received that additional letter from my father. I had no idea what to expect. What he wrote touched and amazed me. Just as God worked in my life, unbeknownst to me, He worked in my father's life too. Here are the contents of his letter:

> Dear Mark,
>
> In 1990 I gave my life to Jesus. Since 1992 I have been involved in men's ministry. Over time I became more and more aware of the impact which my dad had on my life – and I grieved over the impact which I had to have had on your life.
>
> I am writing to ask your forgiveness, to apologize to you (and your family) for what I have done, and to assure you that what happened between your mother and I was no fault of yours. Please forgive me.
>
> I have often wondered if we would meet at a Promise Keepers Conference (or such). If you have not had the benefit of Christian men to help you, I trust you will seek them out. If you have, praise God. My prayers go with you.
>
> In Christ,
>
> Dad

I was alone when I read his letter. After reading it, I could identify with Joseph's weeping. Was the letter a complete fix for all things paternal? No, but it was a gift from my heavenly Father. It let me know God was still at work in my heart and amazingly in the heart of my earthly father too.

God Heals the Heart of the Wounded

For wounded, injured, or deeply hurt people, the thought that God might work in the heart of their abuser(s) can be hard to swallow. Like Joseph, some have carried the offenses of others for decades. It's disconcerting to think God concerns Himself with our abusers. Distasteful even. In one's legitimate anger over being wounded, the last thing a scarred person imagines is the healing of a perpetrator. One might easily exclaim, "Why should God heal or forgive them when they hurt me so?" God's healing work in the heart of an abuser can raise painful feelings in the heart of a victim.

If an abused person discovers that God has worked in the heart of their abuser, it may stir painful memories of the original offense. Sometimes, as I believe it did in the life of Joseph, the resurfacing of those issues provides an opportunity to release pain. As a friend of mine says, "Sin affects us all very deeply on an emotional level." That emotional pain needs to be vented in ways that don't cause harm. In the process, a curative effect results.

As you read through Joseph's story, particularly the later sections when he reconciles with his brothers, profound episodes of weeping get recorded. But why does Joseph weep? Was it the sight of Benjamin, or Judah's changed heart? Likely both.

God heals Joseph as he releases his pain through weeping. The pain his brothers and others caused him was the bad kind of pain, the pain of separation, of abuse, and injustice. The release represented in his bouts of weeping points to the good kind of pain; the pain of resetting a bone; stitching a wound; or physical therapy. Pain accompanies injury, but it also attends healing.

Joseph needed to find a place to vent the pain which he carried alone for so long. That is the message of his weeping. The second appearance of his brothers, and Benjamin in particular, unleashes the flood gates of pent up emotion. For us, God may arrange other circumstances, like the letter I received.

God actively seeks to heal us. However, we tend to run from Him, forgetting He is the Great Physician. Some of us have not wept in decades. Yet grieving the painful parts of our lives may be just what the Doctor ordered. It's a prescription many choose not to fill. Many believers steer clear of the Wonderful Counselor's probing. They imagine the pain of healing worse than the original offense.

Jesus knew the pain of abuse, abandonment, and betrayal. He can relate to us when we pray and converse about such things with Him. He works over the course of our lives to heal us from injuries even when we resist treatment. It took Joseph, the victim, twenty years to get over his pain. It took Judah, the abuser, just as long to come to grips with the pain he caused.

Cooperation with God determines the outcome. Are we willing to let God touch the sensitive places in our souls? Will we allow him to touch the wounds, so he can apply healing? Those willing to risk drawing near, find that God still heals. He heals sin. He heals bodies. And, He heals *wounded hearts*.

Chapter 5 – Study/Discussion Questions:

1. What does Judah's changed disposition over the course of twenty years relate to God's commitment to work in the life of a Christian? (See Philippians 1:6)

2. How does the work God did in Judah's heart parallel the work God did in Joseph's heart?

3. Does it bother you that God might attempt a redemptive work in the heart of someone who hurt you deeply?

4. How does Joseph's weeping relate to the emotional component of forgiveness and reconciliation?

5. How does being honest about pain you caused or pain you received, move you closer to healing?

6. Are you aware of an unresolved hurt you have caused, or experienced, that you know you needs healing? What can you do to begin to mend it?

JOSEPH UNROBED

Chapter 6

Some Styles are More Forgiving than Others – Genesis 45

"To each of them he gave changes of garments, but to Benjamin he gave three hundred pieces of silver and five changes of garments" (Genesis 45:22).

I returned to where I grew up for my twenty year college reunion and stayed with my brother, who still lived in the area. When I arrived, he wanted to take me to see my mother who was hospitalized, her body failing, even though she was only in her 60's. Having not seen her in years, I found myself unprepared for this sort of reunion. My way of dealing with pain was to distance myself from it.

This time I couldn't run. My brother's urgency superseded my hesitations. On the short drive to the hospital we passed a foster home where we once stayed as children. Then we drove by a memorial to the events of September 11th, 2001. It all appeared foreboding. I tried to ignore the trembling in my gut.

Upon arrival at the hospital the combination smell of antiseptic and desperation caused me to stiffen. We made our way to my mother's room and found her lying half asleep, her face swollen from fluid retention. My brother announced, "Mom, look who's here."

She opened her eyes and smiled.

We hugged.

Talked.

Laughed.

She bummed cigarette money off me.

I gave it.

When it came time to leave, I asked if we could pray. She agreed. I prayed, asking God to help her see how much good had come from her life through the lives of her three sons. I left the hospital shaken, yet relieved. God gave me the opportunity to bring a little encouragement to the woman whose mental illness marred my early life.

She died a week later. I returned with my wife for the funeral. The timing of my mother's death made me glad for our meeting the week before. If there needed to be forgiveness, it happened then. I found healing in those moments. Even without directly addressing our painful history, something in our relationship changed. Unspoken forgiveness.

How Could Joseph Forgive?

We come to a portion of Joseph's story where clothing demonstrates its most forgiving qualities. The clothing he gives his brothers in Genesis 45 hides the weight of past offenses. It conceals, rather than highlights their faults. It stretches, easing strained relationships. Joseph's incredible symbolic gesture, of giving his brothers sets of clothing, versus the clothing they stripped from him years before, offers a "fitting" approach to reconciliation. But how was he able to get beyond past offenses and bestow such gifts on his brothers? How is it that some people, like Joseph, find healing for life's painful scars while others become defined by their injuries? What separates those who heal from those who get stuck in unhealthy attitudes or behaviors? Can we make something beautiful out of our personal woundedness, like Joseph does? These questions stare back at us from between the lines of Joseph's story.

In Genesis 45 we see God healing Joseph and Joseph making four choices as he cooperates with that healing process. His courageous example encourages us to do the same.

Choosing to Release Pent Up Emotions

> [1] Then Joseph could not control himself before all those who stood by him, and he cried, "Have everyone go out from me." So there was no man with him when Joseph made himself known to his brothers. [2] He wept so loudly that the Egyptians heard *it*, and the household of Pharaoh heard *of it*. [3] Then Joseph said to his brothers, "I am Joseph! Is my father still alive?" But his brothers could not answer him, for they were dismayed at his presence.
>
> [14] Then he fell on his brother Benjamin's neck and wept, and Benjamin wept on his neck. [15] He kissed all his brothers and wept on them, and afterward his brothers talked with him (Genesis 45:1-3; 14-15).

Judah's appeal for the life of Benjamin proves more than Joseph can take. He desperately needs to release twenty years of pent up emotion. "He could not control himself before all those who stood by him," the account reveals. Joseph has servants standing ready to satisfy his every desire, but at this moment they can do nothing for him. He must release his pain.

Desperate for privacy, Joseph sends everyone out of the room except for his brothers. He creates a safe place where feelings can flow. Joseph's brothers need privacy too. Exposure before strangers would only scratch the surface of their sin. The product of being caught rather than true repentance. The New Testament speaks of confronting offenders in private (at least initially). In Matthew 18:15 Jesus says, "If your brother sins, go and show him his fault in private; if he listens to you, you have won your brother."

As Joseph's emotions gush forth, the volume of his cries rises unrestrained. He weeps so loudly those he had commanded to leave the room hear him howling. News of his emotional distress even makes it to Pharaoh. "He wept so loudly that the Egyptians heard *it*, and the household of Pharaoh heard *of it*."

Picture the scene. The prime minister of Egypt, in all the regal garments of his position, stands before his confused dinner guests, bawling his eyes out. Can you imagine the reaction of the eleven? They still do not know who he is! All they know is that Judah has made an appeal for Benjamin's life and this Egyptian has a meltdown. The awkwardness in the room must have been palpable.

They're probably glancing around for the nearest exit, slowly inching away from their host! They must be thinking that the prime minister has serious problems. In a few seconds, Joseph's brothers will realize that *they* are the ones with serious problems; their past has caught up to them!

Gasping for air, Joseph reveals himself to his brothers. The Bible then records what must be one of the most understated observations of all times, "But his brothers could not answer him, for they were dismayed at his presence." How can we imagine the shock they felt at that moment? The surprise of a long lost relative showing up at your door fails to do it justice. Discovering you have a brother your parents never told you about would not compare. It must have felt like being hit with a stun gun, as each brother grabbed for a wall or a chair so as not to collapse under the shock. Dumbfounded, they are literally speechless!

Don't be surprised if . . .

We should not be surprised if a similar response be the first reaction of those we lovingly confront. Confronting an offender(s) needs careful forethought and consideration. I'm not recommending you embark on a crusade to confront those who hurt you. Depending on the severity of the offense, a wounded individual needs wise counsel on how to proceed. In some cases confronting someone who hurt you may be the last thing you want to do. In Joseph's case, the confrontation took place in a controlled environment with concerned parties nearby.

Even under ideal circumstances, don't be surprised if those you confront with their sin become defensive. Joseph's brothers were staggered. They likely also shared a concern or two about retribution. The same may occur if you feel led to confront someone. Defenses may go up, communication could shut down. Thankfully Joseph experienced a different outcome. He made up his mind to reconcile, rather than exact revenge. This created a safe atmosphere in which the seeds of reconciliation could germinate.

Joseph makes the rounds from brother to brother, ". . . he fell on Benjamin's neck and wept, and Benjamin wept on his neck. He kissed all his brothers and wept on them, and afterward his brothers talked with him." Notice what the Bible says. Joseph wept on Benjamin's neck and Benjamin wept on his neck. The only innocent member of the group, Benjamin, feels free to weep *with* Joseph. His long lost brother is back! No unresolved issues stand between them and tears flow freely, mutual affection plainly evident. Joseph then shifts to each of his other brothers, the ones who betrayed him. One by one he weeps on their necks and kisses them. Joseph leaves no stone of self-pity, no rock of retaliation unturned in his heart. How is he able to forgive so completely those who unmercifully injured him at a young age?

True forgiveness takes a work of the Holy Spirit. Joseph forgives because God did this miracle in his heart first. No believer needs to live under the weight of mustering up forgiveness toward an offender. The willingness Joseph displays flows from God's influence in his life. Joseph willingly forgave because God broke

Joseph's self-centeredness in an Egyptian prison. God began to heal Joseph as his two sons were born and as he recognized God's plan unfurling around him. It will flow from God's stimulus in your life too. The marvel of forgiveness requires a prerequisite transformation in the heart of the forgiver. Otherwise, in our self-absorbed state, we may never find the willingness we need to forgive and get free.

Joseph weeps on each of his offending brothers and kisses them, but the biblical narrative fails to mention their weeping in return. I have to imagine their initial ability to communicate falters. They are still processing the situation. Afterwards his brothers talk with Joseph, but the content of the conversation remains unrecorded. Possibly they expressed their grief and repented for their actions, or, there may have been a conversation that proved shallow and unsatisfying. We just don't know. That's part of the risk of seeking reconciliation, isn't it? We can't predict how the other party will respond.

We know from Judah's speech and the general apprehension his brothers displayed that God has been working in their hearts. Joseph also had the advantage of an inside look at the true state of his brother's hearts. He listened to every word they said while they thought he could not understand the Hebrew they spoke. He heard them acknowledge the sin they committed against him. He witnessed the panic on their faces, the same panic he once knew. He determined to forgive regardless of their immediate response.

And in that sense, the content of their conversation, which the Bible mentions, but does not record, proves immaterial.

A Whole Lot of Weeping Going On

Sometimes in our weeping we receive comfort from those who weep with us, as Joseph did with Benjamin. At other times we weep even if others are not ready to do so, like Joseph with his other brothers. In either case, we should expect emotional content in the healing process. When the floodgates of bottled up emotions finally open, we may feel as if we're falling apart. However, it's just the opposite. As we willingly release pent up emotion, we begin to fall *together*.

I know this may not be easy to hear, especially for men. I grew up in New Jersey. That's not exactly considered the land of the warm and fuzzy. Letting your emotions show goes against the laws of the urban jungle. In my case, you have to add a dose of German DNA for good measure. I felt it less than manly to cry and I had not done so for years. Cultural restraints, not to mention one's unique heritage, may make venting pent up emotion as foreign to you as it was for Spock on Star Trek. But here's the bottom line for all us "boys don't cry" types . . . *Jesus wept.*[25]

Those two words make up the shortest verse in the Bible and yet they contain the most emotional content! In his humanity, *Jesus wept*. He *expressed* His grief. And you think, *you* should keep it all inside?

---

[25] John 11:35

You're human.

You hurt.

Your pain gets expressed, or, it goes internal, eating away at your insides. You can forgive in your head all you want and never feel free. Expressing pent up emotions clears a path for forgiveness to travel from your head to your heart. When it does, you get freer.

Remember, *Jesus wept.*

Give yourself permission to shed a tear.

It's worth it.

You're worth it.

Choosing to See God's Purpose in Your Pain

> [5] Now do not be grieved or angry with yourselves, because you sold me here, for God sent me before you to preserve life. [6] For the famine *has been* in the land these two years, and there are still five years in which there will be neither plowing nor harvesting. [7] God sent me before you to preserve for you a remnant in the earth, and to keep you alive by a great deliverance. [8] Now, therefore, it was not you who sent me here, but God; and He has made me a father to Pharaoh and lord of all his household and ruler over all the land of Egypt (Genesis 45:5-8).

For a person with festering emotional wounds, suggesting God has a purpose in your suffering must sound idiotic. It might even make you angry. You naturally ask, *"how can God be in the evil perpetrated against me?* How can you suggest the harm that befell me contains a good purpose? Did you live through what I lived through?" My suggestion may upset you.

I am not saying that what happened to you was acceptable or that God perpetrates evil. Rather, I am saying God has integrated His purposes into this fallen world. Because we live in this fallen world the odds of experiencing hurt are high. God, in his loving Fatherhood, can redeem that pain, giving it a positive purpose. That purpose includes God being glorified as we depend upon Him in ways we otherwise would not, if we had never been wounded. As in Joseph's life, He may even use our pain to prepare us for the role He has in mind for us.

I currently serve with a ministry to hurting churches. Guess what. Hurting churches contain hurting people. Through the hurt I experienced, I now work to heal congregations where incredibly painful things have transpired. Without the shaping influences of my background, I would be less fit for the role I fill. Does that make everything I went through okay, does it make it right? Obviously not. However, in God's mercy He heals me to help heal others. I feel a sense of calling and destiny about it. Listen, no matter what pain you've experienced God wants to use you to comfort others when they have experienced similar pan.[26] It's the way God works man's free will, and the pain we experience because of that free will, into His eternal purposes. Are you fulfilling the role God has shaped you to fill?

---

[26] 2 Corinthians 1:3-4

Comforting the Enemy

Recognizing God's purpose in his life enables Joseph to *comfort* his former oppressors. He says to them, "Now do not be grieved or angry with yourselves, because you sold me here, for God sent me before you to preserve life."

Instead of a hard, unforgiving heart, Joseph's disposition appears tempered by the recognition of what God did in spite of his brothers' wrongdoing. His brothers were who they were at the time of their crime. God knew who they were and what they would do to Joseph at the age of seventeen. God anticipated their actions and enfolded Joseph's injury into His good plan for the ages.

Do you believe God can or has already done the same for you? Without the possibility that God works in and through personal pain people are left in a desperate strait. I think of my mother who suffered decades of mental torment and physical ailments. She died at a relatively young age. She never released her resentment toward those who hurt her, leaving her in a constant state of depression. I wish I could share some wonderful outcome. But even with the generous long term care of my heroic younger brother and his wonderful wife, my mother never faced her demons. She suffered in silence, eventually succumbing to physical maladies flowing from unhealed resentments.

Who knows if some of the physical ailments we suffer are not the aftereffects of unhealed emotional wounds. Consider it. Physical problems may be God's gracious way of getting us to deal with deeper issues that may be ruining our health. Physical ill health can sometimes disguise emotional ill health. Joseph addressed his pain and went on to live a long life. He faced his pain, freeing his body from the negative effects of unforgiveness. He dealt with his brothers' wrongdoing instead of suppressing it, or living in denial.

Joseph wears a disguise and fools his brothers for a while. But when the time was right he came clean and defined reality, "you sold me here." He addressed the true cause of his pain, but didn't stop there. Incredibly, he comforts his onetime enemies, while not denying their sin, and frames it in God's bigger plan.

Suffering and Sovereignty

Joseph says, "God sent me before you to preserve life." So who sent Joseph to Egypt? Was it God or his brothers? A real struggle hides in this passage for those who have been hurt, the challenge of acknowledging God's role in pain. More than head held theology, Joseph believes God has a good purpose for the pain he experienced. It's a conviction with him. Joseph repeats his underlying belief that God serves as the primary mover in his life, not his brothers, "Now, therefore, it was not you who sent me here, but God." Joseph sees beyond how he arrived in Egypt and embraces why he arrived in Egypt. He does not see himself as better than his brothers. He sees himself as having a different role in God's plan.

What helped me forgive my parents was realizing I had the same damaging capability for doing what they did. Am I above losing my mental health over bitterness and suppressed rage? Am I insusceptible to the selfishness of abandoning my family? Am I capable of living in my own little world, keeping those who need me at a distance? The safest way to avoid falling into sin, involves admitting one's weakness.

While it took years to acknowledge, I discovered I was capable of doing the very things that wounded me. In fact, if I had not received healing, the likelihood of me repeating my parent's mistakes was high. My mother modeled resentment. My father demonstrated abandonment. It was all I knew. The Bible says, "Train up a child in the way he should go, even when he is old he will not depart from it." I'm afraid that works for bad childhood training as well as good. However, God's sovereignty (His authority over all things) plays a role too. Psalm 27:10 says, "For my father and my mother have forsaken me, but the Lord will take me up."

Grasping the implications of the sovereignty of God can be a head banger. Let's try to work it out in Joseph's situation. Joseph's brothers bore the responsibility for their actions, actions they pursued in the darkest moments of free will. At the same time God works their free will into an outcome that will not be thwarted.

And here is the implication for us. Until we arrive at the place where we are at least willing to acknowledge that God has a purpose for our pain, we are left with a chilling alternative: life is guided by the random acts of evil men, chaos, and pointless living.

The story of Joseph knits his pain into God's humanitarian plan to save the Israelites. It synthesizes the betrayal of Joseph with God's best intentions for mankind. The story of Joseph transforms what happened to Joseph into what God did through Joseph. Are you willing to take a chance that God knows the pain you have faced and plans to redeem it? Can you fathom that He waits for you to recognize the possibility?

The prescription for personal healing can be a tough pill to swallow. You begin to see why. It involves venting long held emotions, and, daring to believe that there might be more to your pain than meets the eyes, at least human eyes. But the prescription becomes more challenging as we move into the next decision Joseph makes in the course of his healing.

Choosing to Bless Those Who Wounded You

> [21] Joseph gave them wagons according to the command of Pharaoh, and gave them provisions for the journey. [22] To each of them he gave changes of garments, but to Benjamin he gave three hundred *pieces of* silver and five changes of garments. [23] To his father he sent as follows: ten donkeys loaded with the best things of Egypt, and ten female donkeys loaded with grain and bread and sustenance for his father on the journey. [24] So he sent his brothers away, and as they departed, he said to them, "Do not quarrel on the journey."

If a person's pain is fresh, or extremely wounding, I may be treading on thin ice with such a reader. Releasing one's pent up emotions sounds doable, or at least worth considering. But with fresh pain, seeing that God has a redemptive purpose in the pain might be a stretch. However, if a person knows Christ they may sense the truth of such a possibility. But blessing those who wounded you? I can hear the protests at this point so I'll be less prescriptive and more descriptive. What am I talking about when it comes to blessing those who wound you?

If I had to summarize the nature of the blessing Joseph bestows on his brothers, it would be that he acts in a way that demonstrates his desire for their *wellbeing*. Promoting the wellbeing of those we love seems easy compared with promoting the wellbeing of those who mistreat us. When we speak of promoting the wellbeing of a perpetrator we look past what we think they deserve and give them what they really *need*. Some of us might think they need corrective discipline or to pay restitution; or, to spend some time behind bars! In some cases that is appropriate. But in this case, Joseph goes in a different direction.

He first promotes his brothers' wellbeing by arranging for them to have a place of their own in Egypt. The land they receive looks inviting. Pharaoh describes the plot he has in mind for them as the "best of all the land of Egypt." With Pharaoh's endorsement the Israelites relocate to the land of Goshen. Additionally, Joseph promises to provide for their physical needs during the famine, which still has five years to go, so they will not be "impoverished." The wagon train that was sent to retrieve their families left them little excuse to resist the offer.

We are not talking about theoretical wellbeing when we talk about blessing those who wound us. We are talking about substance. This was anything but a second rate reconciliation. Joseph could have kept his family at arm's length, sending out supplies to them in Canaan every few months. Instead, he draws them close, moving them to Egypt. Joseph sets a challenging example. He appears thoroughly convinced of God's good purposes for him *and* his extended family.

In promoting the wellbeing of the offending party we also see the extent to which Joseph goes in giving them what was taken from him. Powerful symbolic meaning resides in the changes of clothing he gives to each of his brothers. He gives them the very kind of items they stripped from him twenty years earlier. In that earlier time Joseph's coat was a symbol that irked his siblings. Now the clothing he gifts them works to heal any lingering rift.

What more powerful symbolic gesture could he make to communicate forgiveness? Joseph once again goes the distance to convince his brothers that he holds nothing against them even offering Benjamin five changes of clothing and 300 pieces of silver. We might be concerned that the favoritism that got Joseph in trouble, years ago, now repeats itself. Or, it might be, as one commentator suggests, that Joseph was trying to make up for the controversy over the stolen cup.[27] In either case, the symbolic nature of the gifts bears a deeper meaning for Joseph's older brothers than they do for Benjamin.

As if these comforts were not enough, we see Joseph express his desire for his brothers' wellbeing when he counsels them not to "quarrel on the journey." Joseph anticipates something. His existence may cause his brothers to begin finger pointing. Besides,

---

[27] W. H. Griffith Thomas, *Genesis* (Grand Rapids: Eerdmans, 1946) 430.

which one of them will be the "lucky" fellow to tell their father that Joseph lives? Who will explain his existence? (What a conversation that must have been.) At some point the whole story will come out and Jacob will discover the truth about Joseph's disappearance two decades earlier, if he does not suspect it already. The brothers might argue over how the story will be told and by whom. With this simple bit of parting advice, Joseph tells his brothers to let it go. He wants them to let go of their guilt toward him as well as their lingering misgivings toward each other. As they head home with their new clothes, Joseph hopes his brothers will extend to each other, the forgiveness he offers them.

Choosing to be an Instrument of Revival

> [9] Hurry and go up to my father, and say to him, 'Thus says your son Joseph, "God has made me lord of all Egypt; come down to me, do not delay.
>
> [12] Behold, your eyes see, and the eyes of my brother Benjamin *see*, that it is my mouth which is speaking to you. [13] Now you must tell my father of all my splendor in Egypt, and all that you have seen; and you must hurry and bring my father down here.
>
> [25] Then they went up from Egypt, and came to the land of Canaan to their father Jacob. [26] They told him, saying, "Joseph is still alive, and indeed he is ruler over all the land of Egypt." But he was stunned, for he did not believe them. [27] When they told him all the words of Joseph that he had spoken to them, and when he saw the wagons that Joseph had sent to carry him, the spirit of their father Jacob revived. [28] Then Israel said,

"It is enough; my son Joseph is still alive. I will go and see him before I die."

Of all the people Joseph really wanted to see, his dad topped the list. His urgency for a reunion with Jacob comes out in his words to his brothers in vs. 9, "Hurry and go up to my father and say . . ." and again in verse 13 "you must hurry and bring my father down here." He wanted to reunite with his father to satisfy the longings of mutual affection and so the two of them could rejoice over all that God had done in his life. Joseph goes on, "Now you must tell my father of all my splendor in Egypt." Joseph relished the satisfaction both he and his dad would enjoy in recognizing God's hand in their affairs.

When Jacob heard that Joseph was alive and ruler over all Egypt, it was his turn to be stunned. He was taken aback at the news, he couldn't believe it! Only the sight of the wagons from Joseph convinced him that his long lost son was alive and well.

Then we have this beautiful little phrase "the spirit of their father Jacob revived." Jacob's disposition changed. The man prone to imagine the worst throughout this saga suddenly finds hope that something good awaits him. He expected to be bereaved of Benjamin, Simeon, and Joseph but gets all three back! The good news breathes life into an old man's spirit. Blessing replaces bereavement.

Had Joseph been vengeful, Jacob might never have seen any of his sons alive again. If Joseph sought retaliation, Jacob's heart would have broken rather than revived. Had Joseph made his brothers pay for their offense, Jacob's dark predictions would have been fulfilled. Instead, reconciliation *revives* him.

Who is to say what effect reconciliation with those who have wounded us will have on others who hear about it? Perhaps like Jacob, their spirits will revive as well. Perhaps the world awaits tangible proof that this "love" Christians talk about actually carries merit. Who is to say how the world would be impacted by thousands of stories of redemption, reunion, and reconciliation?

Our nation flounders as familial bonds shatter daily. We desperately need to witness remarkable incidents of relational healing, the kind that turn the hearts of fathers back to their sons and sons back to their fathers. We need to believe that it can still happen, that the spirit which revived Jacob can revive ours!

Discarding Old Clothes

This phase of Joseph's life required a different kind of clothing, something more forgiving. His brothers needed to discard their tight fitting, uncomfortable, garbs of guilt. Joseph gave them the clothes they needed to put their past behind them. Joseph himself needed a robe of reconciliation, one that could breathe, allowing for the ventilation of buried emotion. His clothes had to be loose enough to make room for God's plan in his life. And in a sense his attire needed to be one size fits all, to put his brothers and himself on the same level before a loving God.

Would you be willing to address your broken relationships? Would you be willing to heal what the Lord leads you to heal?

What if your obedience leads to more people seeing and believing in God's love? Would you be willing to be an instrument of revival in their lives?

Chapter 6 – Study/Discussion Questions:

1. Are you a person who cries easily or rarely?
2. What might be some creative ways to vent your feelings without injuring others?
3. What's an example of a painful event that you can now look back upon and see God's purpose in?
4. How does being concerned for the wellbeing of an offending party facilitate reconciliation?
5. Is there a situation you currently need to resolve that might require a meaningful gesture?

Chapter 7

When You Have Nothing Left to Wear
Genesis 50

". . . and you shall carry my bones up from here" (Genesis 50:25).

Forgiveness provides a rest stop on the path to healing, however the trail extends farther. An individual may have received forgiveness, or granted it, and still be plagued by lingering dysfunction. Depending on the type and depth of a person's wounding, they may struggle with a host of thoughts and behaviors yet to be overcome.

My painful past left me craving acceptance, affirmation, and attention. It fostered perfectionism, workaholic behaviors, fear, and people pleasing tendencies. My wounds exacerbated my insecurities, enhanced my shame, and heightened my anxieties. My pain taught me to withdraw from authority figures and to rebel against them when I got the chance.

Exiting a severely dysfunctional home sometimes means living with a degree of Post-Traumatic Stress Disorder (PTSD). My family knows that if you startle dad from behind, he'll instantly turn around with a clenched fist. My kids may laugh at my involuntary reaction, but I grieve.

Unhealthy relational patterns also impact a person's relationship with God. If we no longer trust authority figures, because they wounded us in the past, how will we come around to fully trusting God? How do we draw near to a God we're afraid of to find the relief we need?

The devil takes advantage of our resulting isolation, lobbing reverberating lies into the mind. A wounded person may on occasion believe they're worthless, unworthy of love, and how they bore the fault for the abuse they received. These echoes of our pain can surface unexpectedly. When they do, Jesus stands ready to help trace the source of our struggle to its root. He gives fresh portions of grace through the word, the wise counsel of a friend, or, a professional caregiver.

The echoes of pain arise in the minds of Joseph's brothers when their father Jacob passes from the scene. Now that their dad has died, Joseph's brothers worry that Joseph may seek retribution for the crimes they perpetrated against him some forty years earlier. Almost two decades have passed since Joseph forgave his brothers and resettled them in Goshen. However, the loss of their father sparked renewed fears in Joseph's kin, fears alleviated only by Joseph's character and the faith that shaped it.

The Death of Jacob

The last half of Joseph's life begins with the death of his father, Jacob. Many notable events surround Jacob's death and burial in Canaan. The honor afforded him by the Egyptian ruling class, the mourning over his body, and the entourage of Egyptians who travel to Canaan all point to Pharaoh's appreciation for Joseph and by extension for his father. The burial of Jacob binds the nation of Egypt and Israel in a relationship rooted in appreciation and respect. (Unfortunately those feelings fade after Joseph's passing.) Genesis 50:1-14 describes the large number of people who departed Egypt for Canaan reading like a preview of the exodus that would take place centuries later. This earlier exodus occurs under more placid circumstances. It's a moving portion of Scripture to ponder.

What follows reveals the hearts of Joseph's brothers. The death of their father leaves them feeling threatened by Joseph's headship over the family. With his father dead, will he exact retribution? For some men, it would be a fair question. However, the work God did in Joseph proves anything but superficial. The work God seeks to do in his brothers proves yet ongoing. Their lack of faith in Joseph flows from a mindset, a collective inability to believe Joseph holds nothing against them. It fuels their fear that Joseph might now exact revenge. Their failure to accept Joseph's forgiveness may suggest they have yet to forgive themselves. They might wonder, "How can Joseph forgive us for that which we cannot forgive ourselves?"

Just as the funeral of Jacob revives old worries, family gatherings of all kinds can expose wounds that still need healing. The fatherless might struggle through Father's Day or the abandoned might labor through Christmas. Significant holidays and events cause hurting people to get depressed, withdraw, or, become irritable. Joseph's brothers' anxieties rise, but their fears afford God a chance to do a deeper work in their hearts. He wants to heal them thoroughly as He does us.

Relational healing sometimes takes more than one treatment. The length of recovery must often match the depth of one's pain. We may enjoy a new freedom when we initially forgive, or receive forgiveness, but there will be trailing remembrances that bring old feelings to mind. At those moments it seems we must forgive, or be forgiven, all over again, as the case may be. These challenges to our peace surface when we realize afresh the implications of another's sin, or even our own.

Redressing slow healing wounds plays a role in God's ongoing work of making us whole. We should not be surprised to face new aspects of old woundedness that we previously overlooked. Not to mention we have an enemy who attacks at our point of greatest weakness. He prods us, agitating old offenses. However, God desires that we bring every new hurtful realization, to Him. He wants us to acknowledge it, understand it, weep some more if we must, and ask Him to help us let it go.

The Memory of Guilt Ignites Fear

> [15] When Joseph's brothers saw that their father was dead, they said, "What if Joseph bears a grudge against us and pays us back in full for all the wrong which we did to him!" [16] So they sent *a message* to Joseph, saying, "Your father charged before he died, saying, [17] 'Thus you shall say to Joseph, "Please forgive, I beg you, the transgression of your brothers

and their sin, for they did you wrong.'" And now, please forgive the transgression of the servants of the God of your father." And Joseph wept when they spoke to him.[18] Then his brothers also came and fell down before him and said, "Behold, we are your servants" (Genesis 50: 15-18).

My wife's grandfather lived to the age of one hundred and three. He loved the Lord and loved to tell people about the Lord. He attended every holiday family celebration until the last of his days, his mind intact. His great grandchildren knew and loved him. When he died, he left an obvious void in the extended family. It must have been similar for Jacob's clan.

While Jacob was alive, Joseph's love for his father provided a safeguard for his brothers. Certainly, Joseph would never do anything to hurt them, lest he break his father's heart, or, so they might have thought. With the passing of their father, the brothers believe themselves in jeopardy. So they call a family meeting and form a plan.

A message is sent to Joseph relaying their father's last request, "Your father charged before he died, saying, 'Please forgive, I beg you, the transgression of your brothers and their sin, for they did you wrong.' And now, please forgive the transgression of the servants of the God of your father." It sounds as if Jacob speaks from the grave. You have to wonder about the message's authenticity though. Could it be one more deception, manufactured out of fear and doubt? Did their worries motivate them to fabricate the story?

With the death of Jacob, anxiety in the extended family rises. Joseph's brothers are unconvinced of his forgiveness, nearly *eighteen* years after the fact! Maybe communication between Joseph and his brothers waned during the first two decades of their relocation. A lack of communication can cause us to forget the character of friends and family. Perhaps Joseph rarely visited his brothers in Goshen. Only as we spend time with others are we assured of their favorable disposition toward us. We need to hear their familiar voices, absorb their reassuring tones. Imagination and time work against Jacob's sons, fueling uncertainty. This would be especially true if they had never forgiven themselves and Joseph had moved on.

Joseph's response to his brothers' anxiety was emotional. He wept. Why? After all the grieving over Jacob that took place during the procession and burial, it seems difficult to believe it was grief over the loss of his father. Though it could have been partially due to the accumulated stress of his father's passing, he has more to grieve over now. The guilt and fear his brothers still carry may have motivated the emotional response from Joseph.

Joseph grieved that his brothers were still concerned with a forgiven sin that was now nearly forty years old. He wept because their collective anxiety caused them to regress to self-interest. Their request revealed the lack of faith his brothers placed in him. Joseph cries because his brothers bring up a painful issue he longed to leave behind. There were many reasons to weep, and a combination of griefs likely struck Joseph. We may not know the exact reason, but we do learn the brothers' betrayal still haunts them.

Before Joseph gets a word out between sobs, his brothers bow before him and declare themselves his servants. The first times they bowed before Joseph, during their initial visits to Egypt for grain, they did not know it was Joseph before whom they bowed. This time, however, they intentionally bow, conscious of their actions. They willingly fulfill Joseph's youthful dreams. Their body language provides purposeful symbolism. They were brought to a new low over their sin. They admit their guilt, even if veiled by the supposed message of their father. If Joseph's forgiveness could be manipulated, his father's request for family harmony would suffice as a motive. But nothing to this point suggests that Joseph's forgiveness was ever coerced.

The Painful Truths We Learn from Joseph's Brothers

Events can transpire surprising us with issues we thought were resolved, but had only escaped underground. Relationships can operate on a surface level, without addressing what truly troubles the key players. Old behaviors and sins sometimes haunt people. People can behave in ways that reflect old dysfunctional thinking. Time alone proves a weak prescription for emotional and relational healing. This becomes all the more evident if we have not sufficiently addressed the hidden-lurking issues. When old wounds break open it offers an opportunity to secure a more thorough healing, but not without a few more tears. All these lessons flow from the brothers' desperate pursuit of reassurance from Joseph.

The brothers' current fears overshadow Joseph's previous forgiveness, eclipsing all memory of the freedom they had. Why did their old fears resurface? Perhaps living in Egypt was a constant reminder of *how* they got there. Maybe realizing they were a despised minority (Remember how distasteful is was for Egyptians to eat with Hebrews?) played on their minds. Perhaps they realized their status in Egypt was guarded by the good will of someone they had hurt badly. It's likely that the passing years granted his brothers the opportunity to reflect on the gravity of what they had done. The brothers could imagine many reasons to doubt Joseph's good will. They desperately needed to resettle the issue in their minds.

I know that in my own journey, facing down resurgent fears and anger *over pain I caused,* has been a stumbling block. For while I was gravely injured in my family of origin, some of my acting out behavior, the negative way I dealt with my wounds, injured others. I have hurt others and sometimes those I have hurt were not ready to forgive. How do you handle it when you seek but are not granted forgiveness?

Not everyone is as capable of the kind of grace Joseph displays toward his brothers. Some relationships resist healing. I have found this to be the most difficult aspect of bringing closure to old wounds, when an offended party refuses to forgive a penitent offender. In such cases, it seems we face a less than ideal outcome, living with the unforgiveness of one while clinging to the forgiveness of Another. It's a tenuous result that never feels satisfactory. In such cases we must yield our hearts to the Lord in a way that grieves over our mistakes while not condemning ourselves to the point of despair. In the end, forgiveness can only be granted never demanded. When we are on the losing side of forgiveness and an offended party proves incapable or unprepared to forgive, give them space. Give them your prayers. Not out of a sense that you deserve to be forgiven, but that they deserve to be set free by forgiving – when they are ready.

Freedom from Guilt Flows from God's Goodness

> [19] But Joseph said to them, "Do not be afraid, for am I in God's place? [20] As for you, you meant evil against me, *but* God meant it for good in order to bring about this present result, to preserve many people alive. [21] So therefore, do not be afraid; I will provide for you and your little ones." So he comforted them and spoke kindly to them" (Genesis 50:19-21).

Can any gentler response to his brothers' anxieties be depicted? There are so many directions Joseph could have taken the conversation. He could have challenged the veracity of the message they relay from their father. He could have been insulted that his brothers thought he would take advantage of them. Joseph might have acted out of his own pain and laid into them. But none of these possibilities are realistic, except in the minds of his brothers.

Joseph's character reflects God's goodness and experiencing God's goodness provides an antidote for many of the lingering aftereffects of relational dysfunction. His goodness provides the security for drawing near to God when we become discouraged. It helps us find our footing when we regress, giving in to old behaviors and thoughts. It gives us a new source of identity as a child of a *good* God. God's goodness replaces anxiety with peace, reactivity with calm. It drives away negative thoughts, helping us recognize the lies Satan lobs our way. God's goodness was the first thing Adam and Eve doubted in the Garden and it is what restored them after they fell. To really experience God's goodness personally, it usually requires that we recognize our need of it. Joseph models God's goodness for his needy brothers.

He immediately allays his brothers' concern, "Do not be afraid," says Joseph. He sees through their appeal to the fear behind it. By addressing their fear, he makes his father's supposed request inconsequential. He wants to get to the root, the real reason for their meeting with him. On what basis does he encourage them to relax their worried minds? Joseph offers a reason that flows not from his earthy dad, but from his heavenly Father. He says, "Do not be afraid, for am I in God's place?" He may be second in command of all Egypt, but Joseph knows his limits.

Joseph also recognizes God's purpose in his pain. That purpose provides the defining principle for his relationship with his brothers. He says, "And as for you, you meant evil against me, but God meant it for good." Does any other statement in Scripture knit man's free will with God's sovereignty as this one? We do not need to belabor the point, except to be reminded how in every painful aspect of life, God works something good through it.[28] In this case, Joseph defines "good" as the preservation of life, "in order to bring about this present result, to preserve many people alive." Preservation of their lives was the very thing his brothers thought was in jeopardy! For Joseph to abuse his brothers, in the absence of their father, would be to put himself at odds with God's purposes. (As it does over time when we refuse to forgive.) Joseph's response reveals him to be a man committed to God's purposes above personal injury.

Joseph reiterates the needless nature of his brothers' fears. "So therefore, do not be afraid," he says a second time. He goes on, "I will provide for you and your little ones." His commitment reaches beyond them to their offspring, tenderly described as "little ones." In this moment, Joseph alleviates deep seated fears. You can almost feel the burden lifting. The end of verse 21 says, "So he comforted them and spoke kindly to them." Joseph speaks *kindly* to them.

What an amazing scene.

The abused comforts his abusers.

His abusers find relief for their fears from their *victim*.

Amazing!

It transpires because Joseph stands convinced of God's goodness and his actions illustrate it.

---

[28] Romans 8:28

Experiencing God's Goodness

I sat on the platform with one hundred High School graduates seated behind me. Dressed in shimmering green gowns with their caps and tassels, my daughter, sat prominently among them. She graduated first in her class. The next day she would give a commencement address at her graduation ceremony. Weeks earlier, when the principal went looking for someone to speak at the Baccalaureate service, my daughter volunteered *me*. Her logic was simple. She told me, "Dad if I have to give a speech, so do you!"

Waiting my turn to take the podium, I wrestled with the worst case of nervousness I've ever endured. Those nerves etched the event in my mind. Finally, it came my turn to speak and I gave my challenge to the senior class and then sat back down. I still fight back tears thinking about it. Tears well up from more than parental pride over a brilliant first born child. I have four children who all stun me with their maturity, gifts, and heart for the Lord.

Tears well up because after I gave my Baccalaureate address, I stood back and surveyed the scene like a spectator. As I did, it was as if the Lord said to me, "Look what I can do in one generation." In one generation, he took a fatherless kid, the son of a troubled woman, touched his heart, gave him a great wife, and blessed him with four kids who would never know the pain he grew up with. In one generation, God entered the mess that was my life and guided me one stop after another on the path of healing. I'm sure he's planned a few more stops in the future. The final will certainly be where he wipes away *every* tear (Rev 21:4). In the meantime, Psalm 27:13-14 provides comfort, "*I would have despaired* unless I had believed that I would see the goodness of the LORD in the land of the living. Wait for the Lord and let your heart take courage. Yes, wait for the LORD."

I don't know how God will convince you of His goodness, but He will, if you let Him. I've learned He provides many smaller proofs along the way; friends, answers to prayer, unexpected blessings, encouragement through His word, opportunities, provision, and the nearness of his Spirit. Every once in a while he provides a glimpse of the big picture like He did that night at the Baccalaureate service. If you know Him, He actively seeks to comfort you in your pain. Joseph's brothers got the comfort they needed. It came through fresh appreciation for God's goodness, modeled by Joseph. If you draw near to God, He will provide the same for you.

Faith in One's Bones Forges Character

> [22] Now Joseph stayed in Egypt, he and his father's household, and Joseph lived one hundred and ten years. [23] Joseph saw the third generation of Ephraim's sons; also the sons of Machir, the son of Manasseh, were born on Joseph's knees. [24] Joseph said to his brothers, "I am about to die, but God will surely take care of you and bring you up from this land to the land which He promised on oath to Abraham, to Isaac and to Jacob." [25] Then Joseph made the sons of Israel swear, saying, "God will surely take care of you, and you shall carry my bones up from here." [26] So Joseph died at the age of one hundred

and ten years; and he was embalmed and placed in a coffin in Egypt.

We witness Joseph's entire life in the pages of Scripture, albeit with some gaps along the way. From his birth in Genesis 30 to his parting words in Genesis 50, at the age of one hundred and ten, Joseph's life ranges over twenty chapters of biblical history. That's quite a bit of content, especially when you consider he shares the book of Genesis with Adam, Noah, Abraham, Isaac and Jacob. Why does Joseph's life receive so much attention? Besides its remarkable nature, his life tells the story of how God works through the entire breadth of a man's life. Joseph comes a long way from being his father's favorite, dressed in a fancy robe. His self-importance worked against him on more than one occasion. Those days are in the rearview mirror now. His character, at the end of his life, reveals a heart marked by faith, compassion, and selfless love of others. None of that character development came easy. Much of it came through tears. A lot was stripped from Joseph both in his clothing and his character.

The previous episode where Joseph quiets the fears of his brothers occurs while Joseph is in his mid-fifties. Verses 22-26 take place at the end of his life at the age of one hundred and ten. It's been ninety-three years since the story opened, eighty since he rose to prominence in Egypt.

What Joseph says and what is said about him at the end of his life, reveals the heart of an aged believer who finishes well. It behooves us to visit with him a little longer. When the Bible tells us that Joseph saw the third generation of Ephraim's children and the sons of Machir, the son of Manasseh were born on Joseph's knees, it gives us a picture of how precious his "little ones" were to him. This is a description of more than Joseph's long life. It portrays, too, the family life he enjoyed, expressing paternal love to his great, great, grandchildren.

His faith and reliance upon God also shines during his final moments. Joseph says, "I am about to die, but God will surely take care of you and bring you up from this land to the land which He promised on oath to Abraham, to Isaac and to Jacob." We all come to rely upon key people in our lives, a spouse, a near relative, or, a good friend. We cannot imagine life without them. They may supply our physical needs as well as the emotional ones. And it's natural to come to depend on such special people. There were a lot of people who relied on Joseph, but they needed to learn what he already knew. They needed to learn to rely upon their heavenly Father.

Joseph's gifts, abilities, and accomplishments flowed from God's blessing. Now he encourages his clan to look to the Lord in his absence. It's not all about Joseph, it never was. He sees his life in the context of those who went before him, Abraham, Isaac and Jacob. He stands as but a point in time, a memorial to God's faithfulness, positioned between those who went before him and those who will come after. God alone remains constant. His faithfulness will go with those who come after Joseph, as it goes with us today.

Joseph, convinced that God has a future for his people, looks ahead and declares, "God will surely take care of you, and you shall carry my bones up from here." In other words, Joseph could have said something like this, "I am so convinced God has a future for you, that when it happens, take my bones with you!" It would take another 300 plus years before it occurs, but Joseph possessed long range faith. Because of the faith he expresses here, Joseph is included in Hebrews 11, the chapter known as the great hall of faith. "By faith Joseph, when he was dying, made mention of the exodus of the sons of Israel, and gave orders concerning his bones."[29] When Joseph was dead and had no clothes left, except for the wrappings on a mummified body, he still wanted to put on faith! From what kind of character does forgiveness flow? One that has faith in its bones.

Chapter 7 – Study/Discussion Questions:

1. What kinds of things make you doubt God's forgiveness?
2. What do 1 John 1:9 and Psalm 103 reveal about God's heart as it relates to our sin?
3. As you reflect on your life, what comfort for hurts have you received from God?
4. How does God's goodness relate to one's ability to forgive oneself and others?

---

[29] Hebrews 11:22; Exodus 13:19

Chapter 8

Updating Your Personal Wardrobe

"But put on the Lord Jesus Christ . . ." (Romans 13:14).

God has left us a convenient "trail of crumbs" in Joseph's life, represented by the various references to his clothing. Some of those clothes represent things Joseph needed to leave behind. Other garments represent advances in his healing and God's overall plan. In one case, Joseph gave clothing away. In another, he anticipates a time when there will be nothing left to wear. Each clothing reference represents a different phase of Joseph's development. The fact that we get to view his wardrobe changes from start to finish helps us understand how God works during the entire course of a believer's life.

In this chapter we review the pattern suggested by Joseph's clothing and look for similar patterns in our own lives. Our lives may not be clearly marked out by a series of clothing changes, but just as Joseph's clothes were associated with particular dramatic events, we will also discover events that stand out in our own personal histories. If we pay attention to those events, and their corresponding patterns, we may begin to discern the message they contain. I hope you'll take the opportunity to pause and review your life from God's perspective, and apply anything He may show you.

The following exercise can benefit you in several ways. It may help you recognize the pattern of God's work in your life and better equip you for His service. It may resolve long standing issues which you never fully understood before. I hope that this process will be a freeing exercise, enabling you to discern the message God has for you, contained in the twists and turn s your life has taken.

It is essential that the Holy Spirit guide you in this process. This is spiritual work that requires spiritual help. After all, we're not pursuing human insight. We need God's wisdom. Examining our lives to gain insight about ourselves, can sometimes leave us unable to see the forest for the trees. It is far easier for us to see patterns and problems in other people's lives. If we do catch a glimpse of our true selves, we may draw wrong conclusions. All that to say, this process should not be undertaken without asking for divine help.

Life's Patterns

Joseph hits his head on the same wall several times. He endures painful tests in the form of crises related to his position and importance. He endures abuse, false accusations, and unjust imprisonment. Each crisis reveals the condition of his heart. God knew the state of his heart, but the crises help Joseph see it.

The time span God used to work things out in Joseph's life bears noting. While we have a reference to his birth early on, his record begins in detail at the age of seventeen and ends at the age of one hundred and ten. God doesn't rush Joseph. It takes thirteen years after being sold into Egypt for this gifted individual to reach God's purpose at the age of thirty. It took at least seven or eight more years to meet up with his family again. After his family moved to Egypt, it took another seventeen years for his brothers to fully address their sin. Beyond that, God continued to work in Joseph for fifty plus years as he lived out his life in Egypt.

Why consider the span of Joseph's life? Because the kind of patterns we're talking about don't take place over a matter of months. God works in our hearts over the course of years and decades. We hope to glimpse that larger perspective. God knows the day of your birth, the day you were born again, and the day you will die. Between those important dates He works to heal and/or prepare you for your role in His plan.

Let's face it. Conforming sinful humans to the ideal God has in mind takes time. For the theologically minded, yes, we are seen as perfect by our heavenly Father at the moment of conversion.[30] But the working out of our salvation takes place in real time, over the span of our lives. By stepping back to ponder the breadth of our lives, we seek to observe our lives as God sees them.

What might God want us to see through the pattern of events He lays out through the course of our lives? In Joseph's life it was

---

[30] Hebrews 10:14

a hindering arrogance, fostered in his youth. It may be different for someone else. It likely concerns, like Joseph's robes, something that must be stripped away. It could be an attitude or disposition that hinders God from working through a person like He wants. It may be a behavior or a lack thereof that has become an unhelpful habit. It might be a love, a devotion to something or someone that gets in the way of one's love for Him. Perhaps it flows from a wound endured early on. It could be an overlooked sin, or a sin someone chooses to ignore.

Whatever it might be, God needs to help us see it. If it were easy to recognize we would have seen it all ready. In reality it's probably obvious, but we're just not used to looking at our lives like God does. We need to see what He sees and hear what He is saying to us through the unique pattern of events that make up each of our lives.

We don't want to turn this into a spiritual guessing game. If God works to conform us to the image of his Son, it means there are some things in our lives that *need* adjustment. It also means He will put us in circumstances that facilitate the changes we need to make. Like the pattern of Joseph's clothing, our patterns will be obvious. We simply need to take the time to think circumspectly about the course our life has taken and recognize the pattern(s) and the issue(s) behind them. When we deal with the root issues that impede us, we experience a new freedom and usefulness, similar to that of Joseph.

We should notice that some of the patterns in Joseph's life

symbolize things worthy of *celebration*, good things that we would identify as blessings in his life. Other patterns represent *challenges* he had to overcome. Some of his clothes were closely tied to traumatic *crises*. The three kinds of patterns in Joseph's life communicate that God uses a balanced approach in our development. He blesses us as we struggle through life's various challenges. But He never wastes an opportunity to mold our character, whether the circumstances are good, bad, or ugly. He constantly works to shape us, often right under our noses.

Things to Celebrate

There are some wonderful things to celebrate in Joseph's life. Remember how he could interpret dreams? Remember his gift of administration? These blessings remind us how unique Joseph was. His gifts encouraged him as he sought to fulfill his purpose in God's larger plan.

Joseph's ability to interpret dreams was a special gift. His association with divinely inspired dreams began early. Over the course of time God gives Joseph opportunities to develop his gift. His early dreams, about the wheat and stars, were easier to interpret. His whole family recognized their meaning. The dreams of the baker, cupbearer, and pharaoh appear more complicated. So, we watch Joseph grow in his abilities through the opportunities God sends. The Lord gave him the ability to interpret dreams and planned for him to use it to find his life's work.

Joseph's other gift, administration, manifests itself in Potiphar's household. He works his way up, supervising everything except Potiphar's meals. He was in charge of an important person's estate while in his mid-twenties. Then, when he gets thrown in jail, his knack for administration comes into play again, to the point where he runs the entire prison.

His administrative skills and gift for interpreting dreams set him up for his interview with Pharaoh where both gifts converge. He interprets Pharaoh's dream and suggests a practical, workable, solution to the meaning of his dreams.

So the patterns of Joseph's life are not limited to painful events. They also include good things for which he can be thankful. God used Joseph's gifts in His ultimate plan. Your life will have patterns like that too.

You are a unique reflection of the image of God. He has gifted you in distinct ways. Those gifts stir in you longing for expression. They shape your aspirations. They frame your future. Your heart beats faster as you exercise the particular gifts within you. How do you identify your gift(s)? Think of the thing(s) you do with the least amount of effort and the most amount of satisfaction.

Why does the exercise of your gifts feel effortless? Because God put them in you. He created you with a mind suited to your gifts. Your heart cannot help but to discover, develop, and display the unique gifts you bear. God wants you to enjoy them, express them, and use them for His glory. What in your life would you celebrate? How has God gifted you and how might those gifts be clues to your role in His larger plan? Joseph had unique gifts that proved a blessing. So do you.

Challenges to Overcome

Every believer faces challenges. How do you know the difference between a challenge and a crisis? A crisis is a painful *event*. A challenge bears more resemblance to a *process*. We tend to face challenges over a period of time. In some cases, a challenge can turn into a crisis. But by and large, challenges include things all believers must face and overcome.

One challenge in Joseph's life occurs when he arrives in Egypt. He loses his familial status, learns a new language, and takes the role of a servant. He finds a way to maintain his faith amidst the powerful Egyptian system of idolatry. He also adjusts to prison life, overcomes self-pity, and endures an uncertain future.

Joseph's brothers provide Joseph with challenges all through his story. They begin during his upbringing in Canaan, when they despise him. Another occurs when his brothers show up at his door in Egypt and they must work through issues of reconciliation. This same kind of challenge shows up at Jacob's death when his brothers bring up their sin and seek Joseph's forgiveness. Family can provide us with lots of challenges.

Another challenge arises at his death. Though death for Joseph was not a crisis, it was something to overcome. He succeeds in keeping faith in the face of death and closes out his life without a hint of doubt.

Throughout his life Joseph faced and overcame challenges. Had he allowed them turn into crises, by rebelling against Potiphar, trying to escape from prison, or, by abusing his brothers, it would have meant that God had more lessons for him to learn.

Challenges make up a large part of our history and fill out the context of our lives. God knows the challenges you face, just as He knew the ones Joseph had to stare down. If we were to sit down with the Lord, he would acknowledge our challenges and see our lives in their light. In a way, challenges form the backdrop of our lives; the accentuating circumstances that give our blessings and crises meaningful context.

Painful Crises

Of his blessings, challenges, and crises the latter stands out most clearly in Joseph's life. Joseph faced one clothing crisis after another. The coat of many colors was a symbol of something very painful for Joseph's brothers. The coat represented favoritism, position, and privilege. It carried an air of arrogance about it. Its removal was a great trauma in Joseph's life.

The same kind of trauma is repeated when Mrs. Potiphar strips Joseph of another cloak. In that painful event Joseph does nothing wrong. But God sees things we do not and He works hard to get us to see what He sees. The second cloak carried the same scent of self-importance as Joseph's first coat. He says, "There is no one greater in this house than I." He has yet to recognize what God wants to do in his heart so he must go through more pain until he does.

The clothing Joseph leaves behind in Potiphar's jail also speaks of his standing. Joseph may have gained a measure of prominence as the jail administrator, but he was forgotten by the chief cupbearer. His one hope of escape totally forgets him. What greater torment exists, for a self-important individual, than being forgotten? After he languishes in jail two more years, Joseph finally puts his crises behind him when Pharaoh places a new robe on him.

Facing Root Issues

God sought to bring the root issue in Joseph's life to his attention. To do so, God laid out the painful events of Joseph's life in order to speak to a particular matter. God repeats problems, of the same nature in Joseph's life, hoping that Joseph's will identify the cues and discover why he keeps dealing with similar painful issues.

For Joseph to figure out what God is saying to him, he must face the pattern of crises his life contains. It appears this takes place during his last two years in jail, thus accounting for his change of heart. A dramatic transformation occurs between his pleading with the chief cupbearer to get him out of prison, and his total lack of self-interest before Pharaoh.

It might be easier to see how the patterns and root issue surface by using a timeline of Joseph's life. If we drew a simple timeline of Joseph's life, it would look something like this (See Figure 1). In each era I have listed the things worth celebrating, the challenges and the crises of his life. It is a fairly simple chart but what it reveals proves significant (See Figure 1).

Figure 1: Joseph's Timeline

Early Years Birth to 17	Slave Years Age 17 – 27(?)	Incarceration Age 27(?)- 30	Prime Minister Age 30 –	Later Years Age 50 - 110
Celebratory: • Birthed by Rachel, formerly barren • Greatly loved by his father • Dreams set him apart Challenges: • Jealous older brothers • Being younger but most favored • At 17 his maturity seemed in question at times • Managing his father's favoritism and his brothers' hatred Crises: • Brought a bad report about his brothers • Betrayed by his brothers • Separated from his father • Stripped of robe and sold	Celebratory: • Advanced in his work within Potiphar's household • Recognized for his admin. skill Challenges: • Living in a foreign country • Restricted as a slave • Keeping his faith • The daily challenge of resisting Mrs. Potiphar Crises: • Falsely accused of rape by Mrs. Potiphar • His cloak used as evidence against him	Celebratory: • Advanced in his admin. ability and ran the jail • Interpreted the dreams of two of Pharaoh's officials Challenges: • Had to stay in jail two more years after expecting the cupbearer would get him out Crises: • Being thrown in jail. • His old clothes are left behind when he is summoned by Pharaoh.	Celebratory: • Interpreted Pharaoh's dreams and gave him a plan to save the country • Promoted to second in command of Egypt • Someone puts clothes on Joseph for a change • Marriage and the birth of two sons • He shifts the balance of power in Egypt when, in the end, Pharaoh owns everything. • He reunites with his father. • He saves many lives when his extended family moves to Goshen. Challenges: • Implementing the national crop storage and distribution program • His brothers show up (2x) Crises: None	Celebratory: • Enjoyed his great, great grand-children • Demon-strated faith by asking that his bones be returned to Canaan • Lived to 110 Challenges: • His father's death • Facing his brothers' resurgent fears • Facing the prospect of death Crises: None

Summary of the Celebratory Aspects of Joseph's Life

When we break Joseph's life into manageable sections, we see much good that God did in and through Joseph. God's favor rests on Joseph in a way that begins with his father, extends to Potiphar, is evidenced to the chief jailor, and becomes obvious to Pharaoh. He grows in his administrative ability every chance he gets and his interpretation of dreams progresses as well. He succeeds at whatever he puts his hand to. God's blessing follows him wherever he goes. These blessings of life are meant to encourage Joseph as he walks through the various challenges and crises he faces.

Summary of the Challenges Joseph Faced

The challenges Joseph faces are designed to shape his character. He faces the opposition of his brothers; he constantly faces the challenge of being different from everyone else; as one elevated among his brothers, as a Hebrew in Potiphar's household, and, in Pharaoh's administration. The long term challenge was waiting for God to make His dreams a reality. He spends most of that time waiting as a slave or a prisoner. Joseph faces challenges in the death of his father and in then in his brothers' doubts about his character. The ultimate challenge comes when it is his time to pass from the earth.

A Summary of Joseph's Crises and His Root Issue

The crises in Joseph's life are most obvious in the early stages. His brothers heartlessly betray him. He is cruelly set up by Mrs. Potiphar. He languishes, callously forgotten by the chief cupbearer for two years. And at the end of each painful event Joseph leaves an article of clothing behind. The coat of many colors, the cloak he wore in Potiphar's house, and his prison clothes were all discarded.

What was God trying to show Joseph through these events and did he learn it? The symbolism of his clothing remains consistent. In every scenario, it represents position, standing, and importance. Joseph has to let it go. Once he does, the major crises in his life cease. The good things and challenges continue but the crises finish. Why? Because he figures it out. Sometime in his last two years of prison he changes more than his clothes. He sees what God has been trying to teach him and embraces it. Joseph lets go of the self-importance that plagues him. He evidences the change by what he says to Pharaoh. He says, "It is not in me, God will give Pharaoh a favorable interpretation." He betrays no arrogance, breaking with his past self-interest. This allows him to take the next step in God's larger plan for Israel and ultimately His mission to redeem mankind.

Recognizing the Pattern of God's Work in Another Life

To help you put together a timeline of your life, let's take a look at mine. Perhaps my personal timeline will help you better grasp how God speaks to us through the events of modern lives (See Figure 2).

Figure 2: Author's Timeline				
Pre and early Christian years Birth – 18	**Early Training and Vocation** Age 18-27	**Further Training and Vocation** Age 27-33	**Withdraw from Vocation** Age 33-44	**New Vocation** Age 44-
Celebratory: • Hey I'm alive! • My life changed by Christ at the age of 15 Challenges: • Living with a daily sense of emptiness • Wrestling with, "Why am I here?" • Being the oldest son in a fatherless home. • Early, disproportion-ate, responsibility Crises: • Born into a family that would dissolve into divorce seven years later • Lived with parent who languished with mental health issues • Multiple experiences in foster care and welfare system	Celebratory: • College accelerated my personal growth and vocational preparation. • Married my wonderful wife. • First child born. • Assistant pastor – great experience with senior pastor • Spiritual Gifts begin to emerge Challenges: • Vocation clarification away from missions service Crises: • Falling out with senior pastor at the end of my first church assignment	Celebratory: • Excellent seminary experience • Worked on staff of growing church • Family grows with addition of second child • Some healing from childhood trauma Challenges: • Signs of problems from my family of origin impacting my current family Crises: • Felt like a falling out with senior pastor at the end of my second church assignment	Celebratory: • Relocation and church plant endeavor. • Family continues to grow with addition of 3rd and 4th child. • Early success in ministry Challenges: • Stresses and strains of starting a church from scratch. • Transition to real estate business for ten years • Started real estate career with little to fall back on Crises: • Falling out with denominational leader over vision of new church. • Resigned from ministry.	Celebratory: • Recalled to ministry • Helping lead a ministry to hurting churches • Many blessings Challenges: • All the stresses and strains of starting a new ministry from scratch Crises: None

Celebrating the Good

As you can see from my timeline there's a lot to celebrate. For one thing, with God's help, I survived my childhood! For some of you, surviving childhood seems like a given, but, for others reading this, enduring the effects of family dysfunction takes on more miraculous tones. The ability to survive difficult circumstances has benefited me all my life, especially when I started a new ministry or business venture. My gifts and vocational calling emerge and develop in each phase of my life. In retrospect there were affirmations and signs of God's blessing on my gifts.

Facing the Challenges

The challenges I faced are strangely consistent. The stresses and strains of my early years preview the challenges reflected in every new endeavor I pursued. Additionally, issues from my family of origin followed me into my current family. Some of the same family issues show up again in the crises I faced.

The Crises

The most obvious pattern shows up in those crises. Notice how three different ministry endeavors of mine ended negatively. There was a falling out with the senior pastor which was followed by another, a few years later. Then a third similar conflict arose over the direction of the church I tried to start, one year into the project. I blamed the other party in each conflict I faced, the final one wounding me badly. I did not think I deserved any of it.

I found myself out of ministry and needing a job. I entered the world of real estate. The real estate phase felt like my personal wilderness wandering. Not content in real estate, I longed to be back in ministry. God was not ready for me to be in ministry and I did not understand why. Neither did I feel joyful doing real estate, but God provided for us during a ten year period through that work.

My Root Issue

Finally, when God saw that I was ready, He revealed my root issue to me. It took ten years of being out of ministry to get me there! One day, sitting in a model home in a new residential neighborhood, I was reading a book by Watchman Knee called *Spiritual Authority*. As I read it, I began to reflect on the way I related to authority figures in my life. I pondered the strange sequence of negative endings to each stage of my ministry career.

As I did, the Lord made it clear to me that *I had a problem with authority*. It repeated itself three times in my life. I had previously only recognized each conflict for what I thought it was, *painful*. At that moment, I saw both the pattern and the root problem behind the pattern. My problem was submitting to authority, and that precipitated each crisis in my life.

Can you imagine how devastated I felt? My problem with authority went back to my family of origin. With a dad who abandons you and a mother preoccupied with her own problems, what kind of attitude toward authority would one develop? God graciously allowed me to see the root of my problem. He had been trying to bring it to my attention for upwards of *two decades*. Ugh – I am such a slow learner!

When I recognized the problem, I did not simply say, "Hmm – that's interesting." No, I was broken. I repented on a level that seemed to go down to my DNA. When God brings something of this magnitude to our attention, it requires repentance. I had no resistance to the idea of repenting. I *wanted* to repent and rejoiced that the Lord had shown me what He'd done. I rejoiced further that I was free of the hindering issue in my life.

I was free, but there would be tests. There would still be the tendency to suspect the motives of authority figures. There would be worry that someone in authority would abandon me again. It was necessary to keep my radar turned on to avoid residual traits that had previously shaped my life. I still do that today.

To make my repentance as authentic as I could, I went back to those ministry related authority figures, the ones who were still alive, and repented before them. Was it tearful? Did I weep like Joseph? How could I not? The relief was overwhelming. Shortly thereafter, God began to open doors and move me back into ministry, a ministry that helps churches hear what Jesus is saying to them, just as He helped me hear. The changes we see in churches are as dramatic as the change in my life and potentially in yours (Visit blessingpoint.org for more info about our work with churches.).

Root Issue Summary

To figure out what God is saying to us, and understand the why behind our pain, we must focus primarily on the pattern of crises our life may contain. There is a root issue residing beneath that pattern. The pain we experience merely signals the existence of a deeper problem. Most of us mistake the pain for the problem and never address the root cause. We often simply gloss over the symptoms without any real insight.

To figure out the root cause of our issues, we need to ask the Lord, "What is the real nature of the problems I've been facing?" Or, "If I continue to have a problem in this particular area, what are you trying to show me about myself?" Or, "What are you trying to tell me through the pattern of painful events I have faced?" We want to recognize any root issue the Lord seeks to bring to our attention and address it before Him. It requires hard work, but it is the kind of work God knows that we must face.

Shrinking Back

God may be waiting, at this very moment, to heal you from past pain, but you might hesitate to go there. Many people choose to shrink back from addressing their pain and stay locked in repetitive patterns. Their hesitancy to address their pain speaks to the pain's depth. Many are in desperate need of healing, but fear dealing with their pain. That's understandable, but healing requires us to consider any patterns of pain in our lives.

What kind of painful crises are we talking about? The big

stuff. It could be a divorce(s); one or more health crises; the sudden loss of a job(s); abusive or addictive behaviors; or a broken relationship(s). I mention none of these lightly, because I know the depth of pain they carry. To glibly declare that God has a purpose in one's pain, whatever that pain might be, feels uncomfortable to me. But to say that what happens to a believer reaches beyond the scope of God's ability to redeem or heal sounds wrong-headed. Within that tension we can discern a better, larger, purpose for our pain.

Why go through trauma in this life and squander the experience by failing to recognize God's redeeming purpose in it? If "all things work together for good" as so many of us like to quote, that includes the bad stuff. If a person fails to do anything but get through their pain, neglecting to seek God's face about His purpose in the pain, he or she has missed the message the pain was intended to bear. That person may, like Joseph, face another related crisis until he or she hears and responds to Him. He loves us enough to keep these issues alive until we address them and moves us on in His plan.

I hope you'll take the time to prayerfully consider the course your life has taken. Start by dividing your life into three or four manageable segments. Organize each section around time frames that make sense to you. Perhaps you could base them around where you lived in each era, or something else, whatever works best. List the blessings, challenges, and crises in each phase of your life. Then identify and list the patterns or themes that run through the eras. List them. Celebrate the good things God has done, acknowledge the challenges you faced, and pay careful attention to the crises you lived through.

When you get to the crises, ask God to show you the theme, tendency, or key moment that started the pattern. It might be a habit, a disposition, a wound, a behavior, or a sin you have yet to address before the Lord. That thing, whatever *it* is, stands between you and the freedom you desire.

Courage

This kind of self-examination takes courage; courage to be honest about one's pain; courage to be honest about how that pain impacts one's relationships with others, and even with God. Maybe it takes courage mixed with a degree of desperation. I'm sure Joseph felt desperate at times, especially in prison. So desperate, he was finally willing to hear what God was saying to him through the painful situations he had faced.

What does the pattern of Joseph's life teach us? Sometimes we need a new wardrobe. We need to leave our old clothes behind. Yes, our old garments might feel comfortable but if we look closely they are tattered and threadbare. They're out of style for the occasion, at least the one the Lord longs for us to experience – our place in His larger plan. I pray it takes you far less time to discover the pattern of His work in your life than it took me, or Joseph.

Additional Resources:

Recognizing the Pattern of God's Work in Your Life:

1. Ask God to guide you as you start this process. He is gracious and eager to help you see what He sees. You are his child, the object of His love. He desires your personal and spiritual development. Thank Him in advance for what He will show you.

2. Divide your life into manageable phases. Title each phase in a way that makes sense to you.

3. Identify the things worth celebrating, the challenges you faced and the crises in each phase of your life.

4. Review the phases and look for patterns or themes that run through each phase of your life.

5. Focus on the crises. Is there a pattern of repetitive pain in your life? If so, look for a root problem that explains why this keeps happening.

6. Identify the root problem by coming up with a theme, tendency, behavior, attitude, event, wound, or sin that explains the pattern.

7. Was there a point in time when the crises started? This often indicates when the trouble began and suggests its nature.

8. How did your life start out? Often the roots of our pattern of pain start early, as did mine.

9. Once you identify a possible root problem, pray over it. See if you sense confirmation in your spirit about it. When you hit upon it, it will likely be obvious. If you ask God to show you what He sees, do you think he will hide it from you?

10. Share what you discover with a close friend, someone who knows your history, in order to seek confirmation of what you think the Lord reveals to you.

11. If needed, repent over what you have discovered about yourself. Ask for God's forgiveness and healing. He's been waiting for you do this for only He knows how long.

12. If needed, go to people related to your crises and repent before them for your part in any conflict. For especially

ADDITIONAL RESOURCES

difficult situations, get godly advice before doing this. In some cases professional counsel may be required.

13. Look for signs of God's blessing in your life after you address your root problem. You will likely see "God things" happen that confirm your progress and new freedom.

Phase One of Your Life:

What would you title this phase? _____

What is worth celebrating in this phase of your life?

What challenges did you face in this phase of your life?

What crises did you experience in this phase of your life?

ADDITIONAL RESOURCES

Phase Two of Your Life:

What would you title this phase? _____

What is worth celebrating in this phase of your life?

What challenges did you face in this phase of your life?

What crises did you experience in this phase of your life?

Phase Three of Your Life:

What would you title this phase? _____

What is worth celebrating in this phase of your life?

What challenges did you face in this phase of your life?

What crises did you experience in this phase of your life?

ADDITIONAL RESOURCES

Phase Four of Your Life (if needed):

What would you title this phase? _____

What is worth celebrating in this phase of your life?

What challenges did you face in this phase of your life?

What crises did you experience in this phase of your life?

Phase Five of Your Life (if needed):

What would you title this phase? _____

What is worth celebrating in this phase of your life?

What challenges did you face in this phase of your life?

What crises did you experience in this phase of your life?

ADDITIONAL RESOURCES

What themes or patterns of good do you recognize in your life? List them here:

What themes or patterns of challenges present themselves in your life? List them here:

ADDITIONAL RESOURCES

What painful crises show up (repetitively) in the phases of your life? List them here:

What root problem(s) do you recognize that tie your crises together? (In some cases, this may take prayer and time to discern.)

ID RESOURCES

What do you need to address before the Lord?

If the issues you identify are particularly challenging to address, seek the advice of a pastor or counselor who can help you walk through them.

ACKNOWLEDGEMENTS

I am indebted to several people who helped make this book a reality. Thank you to my friends at Carriage Lane Presbyterian Church (PCA) who gave me the opportunity to teach an early version of this material. Your encouragement went a long way in making this book a reality. I have to thank Mitch Schultz who provided valuable editing that shaped the tone and content of the manuscript. Thanks goes to Jesse Barnard for coming up with the title and to Brooke Barnard for her editing and feedback. A special thanks goes to my friend Ken Quick who guided me to a higher level of execution and whose own work is reflected in the historical review process laid out in the last chapter. Finally, I want to express thanks to Debbie Smith who proofread the manuscript, correcting my commas and unhitching my conjunctions. Each person I have acknowledged played a key role in shaping *Joseph Unrobed*. Thank you all!

Made in the USA
Columbia, SC
11 October 2018